IE UNIVERSITY CENTER FOR
HUMAN VALUES SERIES

Stephen Macedo, Editor

of titles in this series appears at the back of the book.

ACTIVE ANI   T

A li

Active and Passive Citizens

A DEFENSE OF
MAJORITARIAN DEMOCRACY

RICHARD TUCK

PRINCETON UNIVERSITY PRESS
PRINCETON & OXFORD

Published by Princeton University Press
41 William Street, Princeton, New Jersey 08540
99 Banbury Road, Oxford OX2 6JX

press.princeton.edu

All Rights Reserved

Library of Congress Cataloging-in-Publication Data

Names: Tuck, Richard, 1949- author.
Title: Active and passive citizens : a defense of majoritarian democracy / Richard Tuck.
Description: Princeton, NJ : Princeton University Press, [2024] | Series: The university center for human values series | Includes bibliographical references and index.
Identifiers: LCCN 2023030663 (print) | LCCN 2023030664 (ebook) | ISBN 9780691242798 (hardback) | ISBN 9780691242804 (ebook)
Subjects: LCSH: Representative government and representation. | Political science–Philosophy. | Political participation. | Voting. | Tuck, Richard, 1949—Political and social views. | BISAC: POLITICAL SCIENCE / Political Ideologies / Democracy | POLITICAL SCIENCE / Political Process / General
Classification: LCC JF1051 .T75 2024 (print) | LCC JF1051 (ebook) | DDC 321.8–dc23/eng/20230809
LC record available at https://lccn.loc.gov/2023030663
LC ebook record available at https://lccn.loc.gov/2023030664

British Library Cataloging-in-Publication Data is available

Editorial: Rob Tempio and Chloe Coy
Production Editorial: Ali Parrington
Jacket Design: Chris Ferrante
Production: Erin Suydam
Publicity: William Pagdatoon
Copyeditor: Molan Goldstein

Jacket Credit: Lambeth Election Nomination, Kennington Park, 1865, engraving from *The Illustrated London News*. Courtesy of INTERFOTO / Alamy Stock Photo.

This book has been composed in Arno

Printed on acid-free paper. ∞

Printed in the United States of America

10 9 8 7 6 5 4 3 2 1

CONTENTS

ACTIVE AND PASSIVE CITIZENS

Introduction

Stephen Macedo

WHAT SHOULD democracy mean to us?

Given opinion polls showing plummeting confidence in democracy, particularly among the young, and fears of populism on the one side and elite domination on the other, amidst globalization and the internationalization of governance and the backlash against them, how can we revive faith in a democracy that is worthy of our faith?

These questions are as difficult as they are important. Democracy is what the political theorist W. B. Gallie called an "essentially contested concept": theorists and advocates contest its meaning because they wish to proclaim the idea and march under its banner.

In these chapters, Richard Tuck—a famous and enormously influential scholar and teacher of political theory—offers an answer that is radical and intensely controversial, yet also familiar and, at face value, rather simple. We need to place our faith in what he calls "ultra-radical majoritarianism" (chap. 7 sec. I), which he locates in an interpretation of the political thought of Jean-Jacques Rousseau.

Tuck is a well-known proponent of the Cambridge school of political theory. This is the idea that while great texts in the history of political thought can be approached in various ways, primacy should be given to understanding their meaning in the context of the time in which they were written and received.

Far from turning his back on that historical approach, Tuck here argues that the best answer to the problem of democracy for our time is the answer that Rousseau gave in his time.

———

This volume is based on the Tanner Lectures on Human Values delivered by Richard Tuck at Princeton University in November 2019. Those lectures were organized under the auspices of Princeton's University Center for Human Values. On that occasion, each of Tuck's two lectures was followed by two commentators—each of them also a distinguished political theorist or philosopher. Both evenings featured much lively debate and discussion, as the present volume amply attests.

The text that follows consists of Tuck's two lectures (chapters 1 and 2) and the four commentaries, all of which were revised and, in most cases, expanded, plus Tuck's response to his critics, presented here for the first time.

In this introduction I provide a summary that highlights some main themes.

———

The contrast between "active and passive citizens," which gives this book its title, is taken from Abbé Sieyès, whose great and enduring influence on the theory and practice of constitutional democracy Tuck regrets.

Both Sieyès and Rousseau endorsed the political equality of all citizens. But they differed sharply on how they conceived of people's role as active citizens.

On Sieyès's view, primary importance is assigned to securing people's fundamental rights to the "protection of their person, their property, their liberty, etc." Rights should be entrenched in a constitution and protected by a constitutional court. People do also have the right to play a part in the "formation of public institutions": by voting for representatives who deliberate about the public good and make the laws that the people live under, without the direct active involvement of citizens.

The result is that in liberal constitutional democracy, and thanks in part to the influence of Sieyès, the opportunity for active control of government by the citizens is attenuated and, Tuck argues, "all citizens" are "in effect passive" (chap. 1 sec. I).

Tuck offers a radical alternative: he defends majoritarian democracy in "rather old-fashioned terms." His defense is advanced along two fronts. He argues first that majoritarian democracy is at the center of Rousseau's political thought, properly interpreted. In addition, he argues for the attractiveness of majoritarian democracy on moral and practical grounds.

───────

Rousseau's "fundamental idea," says Tuck, is "that no law carries obligation for us unless we have *actually* taken part in making it." The people themselves are sovereign and must approve the laws under which they live, not through their representatives but directly, ideally by assembling and voting in person. As Rousseau remarked (*Social Contract* III.15), "Every law that the people has not ratified in person is null and void—is in fact not law." And "Sovereignty . . . cannot be represented. . . . The deputies of the people, therefore, are not and cannot be its representatives: they are merely its stewards." In sum, says Tuck for Rousseau, "the basis of all law must be the general will which is simply a majority vote by the entire population" (chap. 1 sec. III).

In order to be fully free, moreover, the people must possess legislative authority that is unbound by any higher law or authority. The only constraints, it appears, is that everyone's right to vote is respected and the people have access to "adequate information" (*Social Contract* II.3).

The laws that the sovereign people must themselves consider are the fundamental laws of the political community—the constitutional and basic laws—not all the administrative details. These basic laws should be decided by a collective vote of the people, who ought then to acknowledge the decision of the majority as their own.

Is it really possible in our world, as opposed to Rousseau's Geneva, for the people themselves to assemble together and vote? Rousseau "always expressed a strong preference for mass citizen assemblies if they could be held," says Tuck, but if the people could not "turn up in person ... they had to *mandate* their delegates" (chap. 1 sec. III). Citizens must "bind the representatives to follow their instructions exactly, and ... make them render their constituents a strict account of their conduct" in the legislature.[1] Frequent elections (short terms of office) would also help reduce representatives' independence. This is "mandation": if legislative power is delegated to representatives, the people should "mandate" or instruct their delegates how to vote. Tuck observes that plebiscites, a later innovation that Rousseau never considered, are also consistent with Rousseauian principles.

————

Tuck squarely rejects a wide range of familiar theories of democracy. He rejects what are called "epistemic" theories, which view elections as ways of arriving at "independently specifiable right answers" to political questions. And he rejects "sortition," or the idea of filling seats in assemblies by drawing lots among ordinary citizens—as with juries—rather than election.

All of these alternatives lack an adequate appreciation of what Tuck calls the "agential view of citizenship." Only where voting is central can citizens themselves "play a real and effective part" in important decisions and directly "bring about an outcome" (chap. 2 sec. III). Then democracy is "a kind of civilized and domesticated version of a mob" (chap. 2 sec V): mass action seeking to bring about change.

"Active democracy," as Tuck defends it and finds it in the political writings of Rousseau, includes the idea that "everyone had to take part in the making of the laws which obliged them." A natural question then is: what about resident aliens and women?

Tuck argues that not only citizens but all *habitants*, including resident aliens, "must be able to vote for the laws under which they" live (chap. 1 sec. IV). As for women, Tuck says that we should not assume, as most do, that Rousseau thought they should be excluded. He cites evidence that "very many women" voted in local meetings in France between 1789 and 1793; and some, including widows, were enfranchised as heads of households (chap. 1 sec. IV). Rousseau would also have included resident aliens in the vote, lest they too be denied political freedom.

———

Tuck also departs from many others in interpreting Rousseau's most famous passages concerning the general will in the *Social Contract* (II.3):

> It follows from what has gone before that the general will is always right and tends to the public advantage; but it does not follow that the deliberations of the people are always equally correct. . . . There is often a great deal of difference between the will of all and the general will; the latter considers only the common interest, while the former takes private interest into account, and is no more than a sum of particular wills.

Tuck argues that we should understand Rousseau as he was understood by his contemporaries, such as Jean-Baptiste Sallaville, who said, "the will of the majority is . . . the expression of the general will; it is Sovereign; it constitutes the Law. All the other wills should abase themselves before it; and its decrees must have the force of Destiny."

Suffice it to say that this interpretation is controversial and sharply contested by our commentators.

———

Let me conclude this cursory summary by noting some of the practical advantages Tuck claims for his "ultra-radical" majoritarian conception of democracy.

There is of course the familiar fact that the people's representatives and other political elites are liable to develop interests of their own, at odds with those of their constituents: the "Representatives of the people are . . . easy to corrupt." This is part of why people feel so alienated from government. The agential view of citizenship helps combat this by recentering power in the hands of the voting public.

As things stand, moreover, under representative government with judicial review and other "checks and balances," "people are encouraged to be 'active' citizens, and then at the crucial moment their activity is blocked and the action is solely in the hands of their representatives." In our system, voters "are *active* but not *decisive*," capable more of "*agitation* than *action*" (chap. 2 sec. VII). The result is that people are encouraged to form and express their political opinions in an irresponsible manner, without regard to the consequences of their actual implementation, over which they have no control (chap. 2 sec. VII).

Even more strikingly, Tuck urges that we consider the "possibility that an unconstrained electorate might, counterintuitively, be a more reliable basis for civil peace than a system of entrenched rights." Tuck argues that when courts decide, for example, that a right of access to abortion should be guaranteed notwithstanding the existence of state laws to the contrary, opponents may feel intense hostility at being subject to "inaccessible sources of power." When the majority rules, in contrast, and voting decides all basic questions then the "temporary nature of any defeat . . . damps down the violent passions of the losers, since they live to fight again another day" (chap. 2 sec. IV).

At a time when many Americans profess concern about the possibility of civil war, it is worth considering Tuck's suggestion that the political system "least likely to engender the kinds of hostilities that might lead to a coup" is unrestrained majority rule, since it allows "maximum scope for a relatively rapid change of policy" (chap. 2 sec. IV).

While acknowledging that the "social base of a confident democracy has been eroded," Tuck concludes nevertheless that we should seek ways to "increase rather than decrease the effectiveness of voting as distinct from other forms of political action or representation." The force of an "unconstrained and democratic citizenry" is the only thing capable of "countering the enormous power" of "modern capitalist enterprises" that wield so much power over our lives.

———

Following Tuck's opening chapters (based on his lectures) are the four commentaries.

Joshua Cohen begins by noting that, on Tuck's interpretation, the basic requirements of political morality are substantive for Sieyès and procedural for Rousseau. For Sieyès, "the state is legitimate when it both protects" the "fundamental natural and civil rights" of everyone residing in its territory and when it makes "laws that advance the general welfare." For Tuck's Rousseau, in contrast, "political legitimacy is fundamentally procedural: a matter of how decisions are made"—by majority decision—"not of what is decided."

Cohen then sets out a "different reading" of Rousseau's political theory "as a marriage of procedure and substance." This draws on Cohen's own influential book, *Rousseau: A Free Community of Equals.*[2]

Cohen argues that Rousseau's account of the "principles of political right" in the *Social Contract* sets out two distinct basic requirements. First, citizens' basic particular interests (their "person and goods") must be adequately protected; and second, each associate should remain "morally free" or "subject only to laws that 'one has prescribed to oneself.'" (chap. 3 sec. II) The solution to the problem is to be to found in a social compact in which each associate "puts his person and his full power under the supreme direction of the general will" and agrees to be governed on the basis of "their common interests or 'common good,'" using "that shared understanding as the basis for" their own "political judgments." Each agrees "to treat other associates as equals and only to impose burdens on others that they are prepared to live under themselves."

And how is political freedom preserved when one lives under laws made by the political community? As Cohen says, "by sharing a conception of the common good that the laws are required to advance, members are able to achieve the autonomy that comes from acting on principles they recognize as their own" (chap. 3 sec. II). The "general will" is a "general willing whose content is an orientation to the common good." Cohen quotes and glosses Rousseau: "'what generalizes the [general] will' is 'not so much the number of voices, as it is the common interest which unites them.'"

In Cohen's "more substantive picture of the general will," both substance and procedure are important. Both are rooted in the "fundamental problem" of political legitimacy, which seeks the protection of people's basic particular interests and the moral freedom or autonomy that we can achieve by being governed by principles we can recognize as our own. In contrast, "a freestanding willingness to accept the decisions of the majority simply does not solve the fundamental problem, which requires the protection of the person and the goods of each." (chap. 3 sec. 2).

Cohen concludes by arguing that his account makes better sense of Rousseau's active citizenship, and links his plea for the wedding of procedure and substance to Lincoln's description of democracy as by and for the people.

———

Melissa Schwartzberg agrees with much of Tuck's argument, especially his "conception of political agency as realized primarily through the exercise of voting power," and she affirms that this provides "a deeply compelling response to the ostensible paradox of voting." She also endorses Tuck's critique of what she calls "strenuous forms of constitutionalism."

Yet Schwartzberg argues that Sieyès, not Rousseau, is the "more plausible source" for an inclusive agential conception of citizenship. Sieyès provided a more expansive basis for citizen enfranchisement, says Schwartzberg, based on stakeholding, as compared with Rousseau's demanding and exclusionary insistence that citizenship requires the possession of "moral and political capacities." In particular, she characterizes as "a remarkable act of interpretive charity," Tuck's claim that we should not presume that Rousseau sought to exclude women from citizenship.

"Rousseau clearly believed that women did not possess the [demanding] qualities necessary for citizenship," argues Schwartzberg. Here she at least partly joins forces with Cohen: Rousseau's citizens must "focus on what is advantageous to the community" and not simply advance "their private or particular interests." Not every political community will achieve this: "Only in well-ordered communities will the vote of the majority reliably yield the general will," she argues (chap. 4). Rousseau's political ideal of moral freedom is "*morally* demanding—it requires us to orient ourselves through virtue . . . toward the well-being of the community as a whole." The general will requires more than majority rule, and crucially for Schwartzberg, this "is a standard that women, on Rousseau's account, cannot meet."

It is Sieyès, on the other hand, who has "the less demanding version of the general will that Tuck ascribes to Rousseau."

So in the end, Schwartzberg observes that while Sieyès "leaves the vast majority of citizens in a position of relative passivity, as mere electors" of representatives, this does at least provide the basis for a more inclusive (because less demanding) suffrage. Rousseau's more active and demanding conception of citizenship, in contrast, "required the exclusion of whole categories of persons."

So where does that leave us? Schwartzberg concludes that we might think of modern citizenship, with its limited opportunities for direct participation and subjection to many forms of subtle domination, as at least offering opportunities for "passive-aggressive" citizenship: veiled strategies of subversion deployed against the powerful.

———

John Ferejohn identifies three "institutional principles" in Tuck's account of Rousseau, and one moral principle.

The first institutional principle is generality: that "each person should be treated equally by the law" and that the basic laws themselves (which ought to be approved by citizens) must be "general/abstract." The second pertains to "democracy in one country" and the "equal role in lawmaking" of all adult residents, with border controls. And finally, radical democracy: there should be direct majority voting for basic laws or decisions by elected and instructed representatives.

Underlying these, Ferejohn identifies a moral principle of "active democracy": "Each person regards him- or herself as obliged to exercise his or her right to vote actively by playing the part of an agent in making the laws together with others."

Ferejohn then elaborates a series of important questions. In the first part, he "asks whether Rousseau's institutional prescriptions provide much help for Tuck's radical democratic project." He argues that "it is very hard to see Rousseau as committed to either equality in voting or to democratic government." Further, he asks whether Rousseau's institutional principles "actually constrain the government from acting arbitrarily": government officials must interpret the laws and apply them to specific circumstances. Do the sovereign people have a legal way of responding to mistaken interpretations or applications of law, and insofar as they do, doesn't this require a judgment that is "particular rather than general" (chap. 5 sec. I)?

Ferejohn also argues that for Tuck's radical democracy to be "alluring," the people must "see themselves as having the obligation to take active responsibility for the laws" as per the moral principle mentioned above. This is easier said than done, especially in large and diverse modern democracies.

The final part of Ferejohn's comment interrogates the treatment of outsiders seeking residence in the country, and of minorities within, "seeking protection against repression." In line with Schwartzberg's observations on the morally demanding character of Rousseauian citizenship, Ferejohn suggests that Tuck's radical democratic communities must have the authority to "restrict entry to assure that those who enter are suitably committed to common purposes," yet this might be "very demanding and potentially quite illiberal." Indeed, he asks whether maintaining the requisite moral qualities in the community might "also justify expulsions of those already in the community?" Tuck says little, after all, and much less than Rousseau, about where civic virtues come from.

There is much more to Ferejohn's valuable commentary, which concludes by noting that "most modern states are both much larger and much more diverse than Geneva was (even in its mythic past)." What protections are there for "unpopular or unsympathetic minorities"—Ferejohn mentions "religious minorities . . . liberal university professors . . . [and] other weird people"—besides the virtue and "moral self-restraint" of the majority? Is that sufficient for us to cast our lot in with unrestrained majority rule? (chap. 5 sec. III)

———

Our concluding comment by Simone Chambers has a distinct and constructive aim: to defend sortition—the random selection of some office holders from the body of the people themselves—as a promising option in the "toolbox of democratic institutions."

A more complex system of representative democracy that includes sortition, she contends, is a better than majority rule at accomplishing some of Tuck's aims. It would curb the excessive power of the affluent better than majority rule: oligarchs can always make their influence felt in elections.

Radical advocates of sortition may embrace it as a substitute for elections, political parties, campaigning, campaign contributions, and other features of electoral politics. Chambers embraces sortition as a supplement rather than a substitute, yet she maintains that it "radically equalizes access to power." Those chosen by sortition are a "representative sample" of the population and are tasked with making "decisions on behalf of the public at large." A representative assembly chosen by lot—perhaps as a substitute for the United States Senate—would be a "mirror" of the polity in all its diversity, far more so than elected officials who must all compete for money and popularity.

In defending sortition, Chambers argues for equal access to office, not votes. She joins Tuck in criticizing modern constitutions, less because of "entrenched rights" than because elections were "intentionally designed to exclude ordinary citizens from office and power."

And finally, random selection provides "the platform for a certain type of impartial deliberation." Chambers insists that "Repeatedly, ordinary citizens show themselves to be competent deliberators able to employ nonpartisan evidence-based reasoning to solve problems."

Chambers concludes her commentary by challenging Tuck's contention that the agentive view of citizenship "is given full and adequate expression in majoritarian voting in which all citizens commit to throwing themselves behind the majoritarian outcome." Any such "democratic authorization" requires "a robust view of the conditions of opinion and will formation." If the majority opinion is formed under the heavy influence of "misinformation and propaganda," then, she argues, "basic conditions of democratic authorization" are lacking.

In other words, as Cohen argues, the conditions for realizing the general will in practice must be substantive and not merely procedural. The public must be adequately informed, as Tuck himself seems to allow, and the decision arrived at must fall within acceptable, reasonable bounds.

Chambers urges that if we want the whole people to stand behind majority decisions, then the minority must be enabled to feel that "their case was addressed and honestly considered." When that occurs, and only then, says Chambers, can we have a strong defense of majority voting.

———

Richard Tuck gets the final word, focusing on two main themes running through the commentaries. Jean-Jacques Rousseau could not have been an "ultra-radical majoritarian." And, "ultra-radical majoritarianism is self-evidently a highly dangerous principle, and that is why we should not suppose Rousseau to have espoused it."

I will let Tuck's subtle concluding essay speak for itself. He stands his ground and in doing so provides, along with his opening chapters, the most powerful defense of majoritarian democracy that I have ever read.

With respect to the issue of how Rousseau should be interpreted, Tuck lays out the " 'modern' natural law background" that Rousseau regarded with "contempt." He explains Rousseau's debts to Hobbes. For both, he argues, "majoritarianism . . . was important because it was a procedure that made as small a claim as possible to any authority beyond the purely political. It was not the substantive rectitude of the outcome, but solely the numbers of people supporting it, that made it authoritative."

Take that, ye apostles of substance!

And as far as the prospects for democracy in our time are concerned, Tuck argues that as long as the right of everyone to vote is protected, we have less to fear from the power of majoritarian institutions than we do from the popular resentments encouraged by modern liberal constitutions, with their entrenched rights, politically independent constitutional courts, and increasing numbers of international agreements, all of which frustrate the people's control of their collective lives.

Tuck ends with a stern warning: "Appeals to expand or protect democracy will fall on deaf ears unless the power of the vote is fully unleashed. . . . [A] mass electorate cannot be denied its power indefinitely without something like civil war being the result."

Agree or disagree as you will, Tuck's is an argument that no student of democracy can ignore.

Lectures

1

Rousseau and Sieyès

I

The title of this book comes from the Abbé Sieyès's address on *The Rights of Man and Citizen*, which he delivered before the National Assembly on 21 July 1789. In the list of the rights of man, he included such things as "liberty, property and security," freedom of expression, freedom to come and go from the state, and freedom to employ one's "strength, industry and capital" in whatever kind of work one might choose, unimpeded by any "individual or association."[1] (Sieyès was a great admirer of Adam Smith—I will say more about this presently.) But he was not willing to include a right to participate in politics in this list of fundamental rights. He went on to say:

> Up to now we have dealt with the *natural and civil rights* of the citizens. It remains for us to consider the *political* rights. The

I should first thank the Tanner Foundation for inviting me to give these lectures at Princeton in the fall of 2019; in my world this is one of the greatest honors that one can receive. I also particularly thank the four commentators and Stephen Macedo, who was both my host at Princeton and the editor of this volume, for the time and care they have taken in thinking about my arguments and helping me to clarify them. In addition I would like to thank the many people who came to the lectures and responded to them, or who have assisted me in revising the lectures for publication. Special thanks go to Philip Pettit, Melissa Lane, Anna Stilz, Greg Conti, Charles Beitz, Alan Patten, Johann Frick, difference between the two kinds of rights lies in the fact that the natural and civil rights are those *for* the maintenance and development of which the society is formed: and the political rights are those *by* which the society forms itself. It is better, for the sake of linguistic clarity, to call the first *passive* rights, and the second *active* rights.

All the residents of a country [*pays*] ought to enjoy the rights of a *passive* citizen: they all have the right to the protection of their person, their property, their liberty, etc., but they do not all have the right to take an active part in the formation of public institutions [*pouvoirs*]; they are not *active* citizens. Women, at least as things stand at the moment [*du moins dans l'état actuel*], children, foreigners, and those who make no contribution to the public establishment ought not to have any active influence on the state.[2] Everyone can enjoy the advantages of the society, but only those who contribute to the public establishment are like the true agents [*actionnaires*] of the great social enterprise. Only they are truly active citizens, the true members of the association.[3]

This terminology was then used in the first Revolutionary constitution of 1791, drawn up broadly on Sieyèsian lines, in which the category of active citizens consisted instead of French nationals who had paid in tax at least the equivalent of three days' work, were not bankrupt at the time of an election, and were not household servants.[4] It was then picked up by Kant, who used it in both *Theory and Practice* (1793) and *The Metaphysics of Morals* (1797) to make an entirely Sieyèsian point about the importance for all citizens of a regime of rights, and the relative unimportance for them of the management of the state.[5]

I have begun with this passage from Sieyès because it seems to me to embody a profound truth about much modern political theory.

Christopher Eisgruber, Victoria McGeer, David Grewal, Daniela Cammack, Will Selinger, Madhav Khosla, John Wallach, Nate Hiatt, Jacob Roundtree, Dimitri Halikias, Soren Dudley, Jedediah Purdy, Rob Tempio, Molan Goldstein, and the anonymous readers for Princeton University Press. I also thank the John Simon Guggenheim Memorial Foundation for appointing me to a fellowship and providing support while I was writing the lectures.

Sieyès's ideas have enjoyed a considerable revival in recent years, and there are good reasons for this. If one wants to find the first person who theorized the modern state in the way many people now think about it, it would be Sieyès. Indeed, the late Robbie Wokler went so far as to say, extravagantly, that "it may be said that Sieyès is the father of the nation-state, standing to the whole of political modernity as does God to the Creation"!⁶ Because so much of Sieyès's theory is appealing to modern readers, his distinction between active and passive citizens has been treated as an embarrassing anomaly, explicable (at least as regards women) by a general prejudice of his time. But I do not think that it is as easy to dismiss it as his modern admirers think; indeed, I think that the fact that he was able to make the distinction reveals something very fundamental about states of a Sieyèsian kind, that in some sense *all* its citizens are "passive" rather than "active."

The principal reason for the revival of interest in Sieyès is that he combined two things of great appeal to modern theorists. The first, as we have just seen, was his insistence that the primary basis for a political society is its adherence to a specific and far-reaching set of human rights that must be guaranteed to all residents, "passive" as well as "active." These rights should be deeply entrenched, and the Constitution of 1791 made it enormously difficult to revise any article.⁷ It was this feature that led Bentham in his mocking attack on "Citizen Sieyès" to describe the Declaration of Rights with which the constitution began as the rule of the dead over the living.

> We the unlawful representatives of the people will govern the people for ages and in spite of ages: we will govern them for ages after we are no more. The only lawful representatives, the first and all succeeding lawful representatives of the nation, the deputies appointed by the people for the time being, shall not govern them as we do, shall not exercise any jurisdiction over them except such as it has been our pleasure to allow.⁸

In his return to politics after the Terror, Sieyès also began to theorize a modern constitutional court, "a body of representatives with the special task of judging alleged violations of the constitution," thereby inventing the institution that in modern states has been charged with ensuring the continued entrenchment of the fundamental rights.

The second feature of Sieyès's theory that appeals to modern readers was his equally clear insistence on the necessarily *representative* character of the state. Both Sieyès in his writings and the Constitution of 1791 were clear on this: the constitution stated plainly that "The nation, from which alone are derived all powers, cannot exercise them except by delegation. The French Constitution is representative. . . ." And throughout his works, Sieyès insisted that a large nation could only operate through representation. By this he did not simply mean that there had to be elected delegates but, much more importantly, that the delegates had to be free to come to their own decisions through a process of deliberation. As he said in another work of 1789, attacking any idea of mandation,

> The Citizens can put their trust in some people chosen from amongst themselves. Without alienating their rights, they delegate their exercise. It is for the common good that they nominate Representatives more capable than themselves of understanding the general interest, and of interpreting in this respect their own wills. . . . [E]ven in the strictest democracy this is the only way to form a common will. It is not in the watches of the night, with everyone in their own houses, that the democrats who are most jealous of their liberty form and fix their individual opinion, to be carried from there into the public space; only to return to their houses to start over again in complete solitude, in the event that no will common to the majority could be extracted from these isolated opinions. We would emphatically say that such a means of forming a common will would be absurd. When people gather, it is to deliberate, to know what other people are thinking, to benefit from mutual enlightenment, to compare particular wills, modify them, reconcile them, and eventually achieve a result that is common to a plurality. I now ask: should what would seem absurd in the most rigorous and jealous democracy be the rule for a representative legislature? It is incontestable that the Deputies have come to the National Assembly not to announce the already formed will of their constituents [*Commettans*], but to deliberate and vote freely following their *actual* opinion, illuminated by all the enlightenment which the Assembly can furnish to each of them.[9]

In another work the same year, he linked representation to the *division of labor*, arguing that representation was a necessary feature of modernity. We could not now turn our back on the division of labor, which is

> the effect and the cause of the increase in wealth and the improvement of human industry. The subject is fully developed in the work of Doctor Smith. . . . It applies to political tasks [*travaux*] as much as to all kinds of productive labor. The common interest, the improvement of the social State itself, demands that we make of Government a specialized profession.[10]

Just as we do not instruct a plumber in how to fix our pipes, we should not instruct our delegates in how to fix our politics.

But his consistent commitment to these two principles—entrenched rights and deliberative representative bodies—meant inevitably that Sieyès had an equivocal attitude to democracy. He made his name in early 1789 with his famous *What Is the Third Estate?* in which he defended the right of the Assembly of the Third Estate to remake the French constitution, using what often looked like the language of radical democracy: "What is the Third Estate? *Everything*." "A nation could never have stipulated that the rights inherent in the common will, namely, the majority, could ever be transferred to the minority."[11] But the point of this language in *What Is the Third Estate* was to deny the right of the privileged classes to have in effect extra votes in the Assembly. "In any national representation . . . influence should be in proportion to the number of individual heads that have a right to be represented. . . . A representative body always has to stand in for the Nation itself. Influence within it ought to have the same *nature*, the same *proportions*, and the same *rules*."[12] It was not the case that Sieyès even in *What Is the Third Estate* supposed that the twenty-six million citizens of France should determine the composition of the Assembly by *voting* for it; instead, it had to represent their *interests*, and not give a special weight to the interests of a privileged minority. He was willing to say that because "all the States of Europe" are now "nothing but vast Workshops,"

> you cannot refuse the title of Citizen, & the rights of citizenship, to this uneducated multitude wholly absorbed in their forced

labor. Just as they ought to obey the Law like you, they ought also, like you, come together in making it.[13]

But on the very next page he made clear that the "coming together" he envisaged was purely that of "five or six million active Citizens" who in turn "can only hope for a Legislature by *representation*."

Moreover, one can read all Sieyès's works, both in print and in manuscript, without finding any clear discussion of the sense in which passive citizens might also be "represented" by an assembly chosen by their active counterparts.[14] The closest one can get, I think, is his account of how the assembly should consult the common interest of all the citizens, and in that sense "represent" them all, but the mechanisms which he proposed to ensure adequate deliberation were expressly designed to admit of very little control by the population. But given his fundamental commitments, this is not surprising: while both bodies of rights and representation were, on his view, integral to civil life *as such*, electoral mechanisms were (so to speak) *epiphenomenal*, of practical but not fundamental significance—they were a kind of safeguard to ensure that the realm of human rights was protected from attack. This is why I said that the category of passive citizen should not simply be seen as a regrettable concession to the prejudices of Sieyès's time: the rights that the passive citizens enjoyed were what really mattered, and the fact that they lacked an *active* role in shaping their politics was relatively unimportant, since very little of significance for the general population would in the end require this kind of active involvement. If everyone was represented, and no one's opinion about a political question could have a direct role in shaping the answer, then, as I said, all citizens were in effect passive.

II

Sieyès was the great theorist of the kind of state that finally emerged from the French Revolution, and of which he had in part been the actual author. The post-Napoleonic states of the nineteenth century exhibited just this combination of entrenched rights, representation, and a belief that their institutions corresponded to a "general will" without a commitment to ensuring that the generality of their citizens actually participated in *creating* the will. This was the state that

Benjamin Constant praised, agreeing entirely with Sieyès about the necessary link between the modern economy with its division of labor, and political representation;[15] it was the state for which Hegel provided the most elaborate philosophical justification, and it was the state that Marx denounced for its anti-democratic character, with both Hegel and Marx seeing clearly Sieyès's role in its creation.[16]

For a time, this post-Napoleonic state was occluded by the rise of universal suffrage and of various kinds of more direct and widespread democracy. The history of referendums in France neatly illustrates this constantly shifting balance. Sieyès's opponents among both the Jacobins and the Girondins were committed to them, but they disappeared after the fall of Napoleon. They were revived for a time under Napoleon III, and though his use of them has often been seen as an argument against referendums, the Second Empire undoubtedly belonged, in a distorted form, to a general democratic moment in European history, manifested most strikingly by what succeeded it for two months in Paris in 1871! Referendums were then abandoned, until they were revived under the Fifth Republic, which has used them not infrequently. During the twentieth century, they also became the norm for constitutional ratification in a large number of states. But the Sieyèsian ideal never vanished, and most modern theories of democracy fit much more closely onto a Sieyèsian state than they do onto (let us say) the Paris Commune. And some major modern states, for example, have expressly abjured popular participation in fundamental constitution-making—this is true of both Germany and India. We have been living for some years now in a world where the old theoretical defenses of a more radical democracy have worn extremely thin, and to do as I propose to do in these chapters— that is, to defend majoritarian democracy in (I think) rather old-fashioned terms—now seems extremely quixotic.

Marx, who was an extremely acute historian of the French Revolution, put his finger on the reason for this uneasy relationship between democracy and the Sieyèsian state in a remarkable passage in *The Holy Family*.

Robespierre, Saint-Just and their party fell because they confused the ancient, *realistic-democratic commonweal* based on *real slavery* with the *modern spiritualistic-democratic representative state*, which is based on *emancipated slavery, bourgeois society*. What a terrible illusion it is to have to recognise and sanction in the *rights of man* modern bourgeois society, the society of industry, of universal competition, of private interest freely pursuing its aims, of anarchy, of self-estranged natural and spiritual individuality, and at the same time to want afterwards to annul the *manifestations of the life* of this society in particular individuals and simultaneously to want to model the *political head* of that society in the manner of antiquity!

The illusion appears tragic when Saint-Just, on the day of his execution, pointed to the large table of the *Rights of Man* hanging in the hall of the *Conciergerie* and said with proud dignity: "*C'est pourtant moi qui ai fait cela*". It was just this table that proclaimed the *right* of a *man* who cannot be the man of the ancient commonweal any more than his *economic* and *industrial* conditions are those of ancient times.[17]

Marx and Engels in the 1840s viewed themselves as the standard-bearers of radical democracy, supporting every movement (such as the Chartists) that sought to expand the franchise; this was the chief complaint of the Prussian censors in 1843, that Marx's "ultra-democratic opinions [and *not* his socialist leanings] are in utter contradiction to the principles of the Prussian State."[18] If they had predecessors, they themselves believed, they were only to be found in the Babeufists, and even the Babeufists had many faults. But Marx and Engels did have a predecessor, I think, though like many of their generation they failed fully to recognize him, for reasons I will discuss presently. This was Rousseau.[19]

III

It is clear that Sieyès's insistence on the necessarily representative character of the state was a deliberate rejection of Rousseau—who had famously said that

> Sovereignty . . . cannot be represented; it lies essentially in the general will, and will does not admit of representation. . . . The deputies of the people, therefore, are not and cannot be its representatives: they are merely its stewards, and can carry through no definitive acts.[20]

Despite this, there has been a tendency in modern scholarship on Sieyès to assimilate him to Rousseau.[21] This is partly because Sieyès's "democratic opinions" have been exaggerated, but more that Rousseau's account of democracy has been regularly misunderstood.

The early readers of Rousseau were generally in agreement about what he had said in *The Social Contract* and its ancillary works,[22] whether they were hostile to his views or sympathetic to them. They took him to have argued that the basis of all law must be a general will that is simply a majority vote by the entire population. So obvious was this to them that one of his hostile readers, Guillaume François Berthier, reproved him for *not* saying what later interpreters often thought he had said, that the general will was a kind of bearer of reason that could be detached from voting. What he should have done, Berthier said, was to "compare *the general will*, in a community of a people, to the light of pure and unspotted [*saine*] reason in each man taken by themselves. This pure and unspotted reason is *always right*, always inclines to the true good, and proposes what is of greatest advantage." But instead he had simply supposed that it was created "by means of general assemblies of all the people, and by way of adding votes."[23] The same was said by one of his most sympathetic readers: writing about the Third Estate in the weeks before it met[24] in a genuinely and explicitly Rousseauian fashion (unlike Sieyès), Jean-Baptiste Salaville proclaimed that "the will of the majority is . . . the expression of the general will; it is the Sovereign; it constitutes the Law. All the other wills should abase themselves before it; and its decrees must have the force of Destiny."[25] And he made clear that the deputies of the Third Estate should be chosen by the votes of the twenty-three million citizens, proposing even a weighted system in which larger districts counted for more in the Assembly than smaller ones.[26]

The idea that Rousseau was not a radical democrat of this kind appeared first (I have argued elsewhere) in a work by Paul Philippe Gudin de la Brenellerie boldly entitled *Supplément au Contract Social*, and clearly intended as a counter-revolutionary reading of Rousseau.[27] In it, he asserted:

Whatever form the legislative assembly of a nation takes, whether it is all the people or their representatives, what matters is that the laws that it passes should be the expression of the *general will*, and not of one party which dominates the assembly.

> The majority [*pluralité*] of votes never expresses anything but the will of the most numerous party; but that party is not always that of the generality [*généralité*] of the citizens.

And he went on to say:

> *Equality of rights, justice in everything*; these are the signs by which the citizens can always recognize whether the laws that are proposed come from the general will, or from the wills of a party that has seized the majority of votes.[28]

Having argued this, he easily assimilated Rousseau to Sieyès and, even more strikingly, to the physiocrats and their idea that a state should be governed according to the principles of reason—despite the fact that in his famous letter to Mirabeau, Rousseau himself had expressly linked physiocracy to despotism. As I showed, Gudin's reading was picked up in Germany and became extremely influential there, but it is clear that Gudin was pushing against the earlier, commonsense reading of Rousseau's text, and that the link he constructed between Rousseau and the physiocrats would have astonished the author of *The Social Contract*.

Nevertheless, the idea that Rousseau was not in fact a theorist of what we might call "active" democracy is still very widespread, so I want to deal with it in some detail. The first point to make is a familiar one, but it needs to be emphasized: Rousseau's fundamental idea was that no law carries obligation for us unless we have *actually* taken part in making it (what "taking part" means is, of course, an important question, to which I will return below and again in my second chapter). In book III chapter 15 of *The Social Contract*, he said that "Every law the people has not ratified in person is null and void—is, in fact, not a law," and he put it even more plainly in his *Considerations on the Government of Poland*, dealing with the question of whether there should be a concurrent upper house in the Polish Sejm.

> [T]he law of nature, that holy and imprescriptible law, which speaks to the heart and reason of man, does not permit legislative authority to be thus restricted [by the concurrence of a senate],

nor does it allow laws to be binding on anyone who has not voted for them in person, like the deputies [*nonces*], or at least through representatives, like the body of the nobility. This sacred law cannot be violated with impunity.[29]

What Rousseau understood by "law," we should remember, is not quite the same as its normal meaning; as I argued in my book *The Sleeping Sovereign*, where I traced the distinction Rousseau consistently drew between "sovereign" and "government," the laws that we have to ratify in person are fundamental ones, closer to constitutional articles than to the day-to-day business of a Parliament or Congress. In particular, they have to be general *in scope* as well as general in origin. It was this distinction that enabled the French revolutionaries who wanted plebiscitary ratification of their constitutional proposals to view themselves as Rousseauian, while it was also what Sieyès denied, since he believed that *constitutions* as well as all other laws have to be made by representatives freely deliberating.

In the *Considerations*, Rousseau was, of course, dealing with the existing Polish constitution, in which only the—admittedly large—class of *noblesse* voted for the Sejm; the rest of the population, as he understood it, were serfs who lacked personal liberty and were like the slaves or conquered peoples described in book I chapter 4 of *The Social Contract*, who were still, in effect, in a state of war with their masters.[30] The fact that only the nobility were free does not contradict his general principle—that for free men, the law has to be something that they voted for. Rousseau believed that the Polish serfs should be freed, but he recognized the substantial difficulties in doing so; his attitude towards them rather resembles his attitude towards the slaves of British America. Quizzed by a British abolitionist in 1776 about whether it was appropriate to support the colonists when they were slave owners, Rousseau replied that he was confident that the slaves would soon be freed, and that it was important not to undermine the Americans' struggle for liberty.[31] So, although it has been said that Rousseau's exclusion of the serfs from the Polish state revealed the limits of his democratic imagination,[32] I think that is misleading: he was concerned with the kind of obligation to the laws that a free man might be under, and not with the kind of submission to power that a slave might be forced to make. And his view was clearly that the free men of Poland had to take part personally in the making of law.

This did not mean that they all had to turn up in person to the legislative assembly, but it did mean that they had to *mandate* their delegates. It is often forgotten that Rousseau's hostility to representation was not in fact hostility to the use of delegates, if that were necessary in a large country like Poland, though, of course, he always expressed a strong preference for mass citizen assemblies if they could be held; as he wrote in *Poland*, "Representatives of the people are . . . easy to corrupt; and it rarely happens that they are not so corrupted." But he continued,

> I see two means of preventing this terrible evil of corruption, which turns the organ of freedom into the instrument of slavery.
>
> The first . . . is to have the diets elected frequently, for if the representatives are often changed it is more costly and difficult to seduce them. On this point your constitution is better than that of Great Britain . . .
>
> The second means is to bind the representatives to follow their instructions exactly, and to make them render their constituents a strict account of their conduct in the diet. In this respect I can only marvel at the negligence, the carelessness and, I would even venture to say, the stupidity of the English nation, which, after having armed its deputies with supreme power, has added no brake to regulate the use they may make of that power throughout the seven years of their mandate.[33]

Rousseau was perfectly aware of the fact that his ideas could apply to a modern state, despite his preference for city republics; indeed, in addressing the citizens of Geneva in the Ninth Letter from the Mountain, he anticipated Sieyès in his awareness of the nature of modernity.

> Ancient Peoples are no longer a model for modern ones; they are too alien to them in every respect. You above all, Genevans, keep your place. . . . You are neither Romans, nor Spartans; you are not even Athenians. . . . You are Merchants, Artisans, Bourgeois, always

occupied with their private interests, with their work, with their trafficking, with their gain.[34]

When the French writers debated mandation in 1788–89, they had had the passage from the *Considerations* in front of them since 1782, when they was first published. As I observed in *The Sleeping Sovereign*, it is curious that Rousseau nowhere considered the favorite solution of the French radicals to the problem of participation in a large country, namely the plebiscite, but it was only in the year of Rousseau's death, in 1778, that such a thing was tried anywhere—in Massachusetts as it happens. And even after the introduction of plebiscites, radicals continued to look to mandation as the means of mass participation— Marx, for example, praised the provisional constitution produced in the Paris Commune for specifying that "each delegate [to the National Delegation] [had] to be at any time revocable and bound by the *mandat imperatif* of his constituents."[35] Mandation had actually been much more common in the political life of pre-revolutionary Europe than we often realize; MPs in England were frequently mandated by the same gatherings in which they were elected (something of which Rousseau was apparently unaware),[36] and delegates to the Estates-General in France had traditionally arrived with *cahiers de doleance* voted on by their constituents.[37]

IV

If Rousseau genuinely believed that all free men had personally to take part in the making of law if the laws were to carry any obligation for them, an obvious question is the familiar one: did they have to be *men*? And furthermore, did they have to be *citizens*—as distinct from resident aliens—who were not serfs or slaves? If so, then for all the rhetoric of participation, Rousseau was not proposing anything very different in practice from Sieyès; and, indeed, his theory would be less consistent than Sieyès's, since Sieyès did not believe that his passive citizens were under some different kind of obligation to the laws from that of the active citizen: all that mattered to both active and passive citizens was that their rights were secure and their interests represented.

The standard answer to these questions has been that Rousseau certainly assumed that women were not full citizens, and it has been supposed that he thought the same about foreigners. But these are more difficult issues than they seem at first sight. Helena Rosenblatt has called on us, for example, to be cautious about how we interpret Rousseau's remarks about women in the *Letter to D'Alembert*, which was firmly rooted in Genevan social conflicts,[38] but few people have been willing to suppose that *citoyen* in Rousseau's political writings also denotes *citoyenne* and *habitant* (resident alien). Nevertheless, we have good evidence that he certainly believed that all *habitants* should be citizens, and there are reasons not to presume that he excluded women.

He addressed the question of *habitants* in *The Social Contract* book IV chapter 2:

> If there are opponents outside the social compact [*lors du pacte social*], their opposition does not invalidate it but merely prevents them from being included in it; they are foreigners among the citizens. When the State is instituted, residence constitutes consent; to dwell within its territory is to submit to its sovereignty. This should of course be understood as applying to a free state; for elsewhere family, goods, lack of a refuge, necessity, or violence may detain a resident [*habitant*] in a country against his will; and then his dwelling there no longer by itself implies his consent to the contract or to its violation.[39]

At first glance, this might seem to be rather like Locke's well-known argument in the *Second Treatise* that voluntary residence in a country expresses tacit consent to its laws. But in Locke's case, tacit consent was to be distinguished from express consent, a formal act of association that gave the person taking it full rights of citizenship; this distinction was critical to his whole political project, since it allowed him to say that Catholics (who would not take the oath of allegiance, which he clearly had in mind, since it required them to abjure papal authority) were like foreigners in their own land and could be excluded from citizenship—and this would apply to a Catholic monarch. But Rousseau did not say this: the plain reading of the passage is that anyone who resides in a free state has given consent to *the contract*, and not merely to the laws promulgated by the contractors. That is, they are full members of the state, since there is no other way of signing up to the contract than residence in such a state.

That this is what he thought is confirmed by a remark in his *History of Geneva*.[40] As we all know, Rousseau repeatedly said that Geneva was (or, more properly, had been) the model for *The Social Contract*.[41] And in the *History*, he looked back nostalgically to the period in the city's history when it was "as democratic as was possible."[42]

> [T]here was no inequality of rights in the Bourgeoisie. For at that time the difference between Citizens and Bourgeois did not exist [footnote: The word *citizen*, which one finds in ancient acts is only a literal translation of the word *cives*, and has no other meaning than that of the word *Bourgeois*, which cannot be rendered in Latin] and everyone could equally attain offices. Nevertheless there were *habitants* who were not bourgeois; newcomers were not supposed at first to share the rights of the children of the house. But the sons of the *habitants* became bourgeois by their birth, and the word *natif* was no more known than that of citizen.
>
> Sometimes even the *habitants* entered into the General Council, above all when it was composed only of heads of families; for then all who were heads entered into it indiscriminately.

The legal categories in the Geneva of Rousseau's day were *citoyen*, with full voting rights in the General Council (the biannual meeting to vote in legislation and elect magistrates) and the right to stand for election; *bourgeois*, a new resident who paid a sum to be allowed to vote and have some economic privileges (the relic of a guild system of the kind familiar in cities across Europe) but could not stand for office; *habitant*, who was simply a resident alien; and *natif*, the son of a *habitant*. As can be seen from this passage, however, Rousseau believed that in the great days of the democracy, none of these distinctions applied and, in particular, that resident aliens had been able to play a full part in its proceedings.

The belief that resident aliens must be able to vote for the laws under which they lived was in some respects a touchstone of whether or not someone subscribed to what I am calling "active democracy." We find it accordingly in Jeremy Bentham (who once said that he had been fascinated by Rousseau "to the highest pitch of fascination"),[43] who argued in his *Plan of Parliamentary Reform* that "aliens" should have the vote (though he added that their numbers were likely to be so few that "though they were all enemies, no sensible practical mischief could ensue").[44] We find it in the Paris Commune, where a resident alien, Leó Frankel, was famously elected to the central committee and became the minister of labor, something praised by Marx—"The Commune admitted all foreigners to the honor of dying for an immortal cause."[45] And we find it in the early United States, something I will return to in my second chapter. If it was true that everyone had to take part in the making of the laws that obliged them, then this was an inevitable conclusion to draw.

As for women, the question of what Rousseau thought has been compromised by the widespread assumption that the kinds of constraints on women's political activity that were characteristic of almost all countries in the nineteenth century had been in place for centuries, and that anyone who thought that women should be able to vote therefore had to say so *explicitly*. But as we are now beginning to understand, the actual history is much more complicated and remarkable. We have, in fact, an extremely good piece of evidence for this, from precisely the moment I am concerned with. When the Estates-General were summoned in 1789 for the first time since 1614, the rules for election to the Third Estate specified that the electors should be "*habitants* . . . born in France or naturalized, aged twenty-five or over, with a permanent address [*domiciliés*] and included on the tax rolls."[46] Although even distinguished historians such as François Furet have assumed that this meant male *habitants*,[47] it is clear from detailed work on the *cahiers* produced by the local meetings of voters that very many women participated—in some parishes in the Périgord, which has been most closely studied, up to one-fifth of voters were women. In most places it was heads of households who were on the tax rolls and who were called to vote, but heads of households could frequently be women, especially (but not exclusively) widows, and in some places other female members of the household voted.[48] To a very high degree, the last Estates-General was elected on the basis of near universal suffrage, something not merely countenanced but positively welcomed by the royal government and the Assembly of Notables that was advising it.[49] Not until the constitutional proposals of 1793 did women *lose* the vote in France—and we now know that in the plebiscite on the new constitution that was to take away their vote, many women voted under the old rules, for the last time until 1945.[50]

Eighteenth-century France was by no means unusual in this respect: in England before the so-called Great Reform Act of 1832, women who met the various property qualifications could—and did—vote, though not in numbers comparable to French women in 1789.[51] Again, English women lost the vote in 1832. And if we look at the other nations in which Rousseau was interested, Corsica was famous for having full female suffrage,[52] and it has even been alleged that noblewomen in Poland took part in the Sejms.[53] In Geneva itself, however, this seems not to have been the case—though the ubiquity of the principle in Western Europe that heads of households could include widows, and the fact that they so often took part in political activity alongside men, would suggest that if it was not so in Geneva then the city was rather unusual. How would the economic interests of the often sizable concerns headed by widows have been represented on the General Council if widows were excluded? Widows were certainly enrolled on the register of *habitants*, something Rousseau must have known when he praised the fact that *habitants* had once voted on the General Council.[54]

V

If all this is correct, then there is no reason not to think that Rousseau genuinely believed in universal participation as a basis for a legal order. And those who took some inspiration from him clearly thought the same; Bentham, to use him again as an example, produced one of the most powerful defenses of female suffrage in his "*Projet* of a Constitutional Code for France," which was targeted precisely at the active/passive citizen distinction written into the Constitution of 1791.[55] While another of the advocates of female suffrage at this moment, Pierre Guyomar, a faithful Rousseauian, said expressly in 1793 that "in my opinion women ought to be included in *The Social Contract*."[56] However, this has not been enough for many modern readers of Rousseau. As has been the case since the 1790s, the interpretation of

Rousseau has tracked the general changes in political attitudes: thus Gudin reinterpreted him as a kind of Sieyèsian physiocrat; and the Hegelians, as the theorist of a general will detachable from democratic processes. Late-nineteenth-century socialists such as Jean Jaurès rediscovered him as a democratic socialist,[57] postwar anti-communists saw him as the theoretician of "totalitarian democracy"[58] and late-twentieth-century liberals welcomed him as someone whose ideas were at least compatible with those of John Rawls.[59] One of Rousseau's most seductive qualities is that we can all see in him what we want to find (rather like the Martians in Ray Bradbury's *Martian Chronicles*).

From two directions, modern readers have called into question the radical character of Rousseau's democratic theory. One direction is that pioneered by Gudin: on this view, Rousseau's "general will" represents the general good and is, in principle, detachable from the actual process of voting—so that a vote can in effect be nullified if it clashes with what is independently specifiable as the common interest. The other direction was actually first hinted at (I think) by Kenneth Arrow in his *Social Choice and Individual Values* in 1951 but has since become very popular:[60] it is the idea that the general will is authoritative because it is an instance of "epistemic democracy," in which a large number of people asked a question about something will tend to cluster in their answers round the correct one. While this preserves the point of voting, it still presumes that there is a correct answer to a political question, and that it is the *correctness* of the answer, and not the fact that it was *voted* for, that makes the outcome authoritative. Neither view sits very well with a commitment to universal suffrage; this is obviously true of the first, but it is also true of the second, since *universality* has no special role in an epistemic theory: a large number is enough to give us the correct result, and adding votes beyond that number will not make any significant difference and may represent a disutility. But both, I think, are hard to square with Rousseau's actual texts.

The first view largely rests on the most famous and important passage in *The Social Contract*, book II chapter 3.

It follows from what has gone before that the general will is always right and tends to the public advantage; but it does not follow that the deliberations of the people are always equally correct. Our will is always for our own good, but we do not always see what that is; the people is never corrupted, but it is often deceived, and on such occasions only does it seem to will what is bad.

There is often a great deal of difference between the will of all and the general will; the latter considers only the common interest, while the former takes private interest into account, and is no more than a sum of particular wills: but take away from these same wills the pluses and minuses that cancel one another, and the general will remains as the sum of the differences.

To this, people often add the passage in book II chapter 6 in which Rousseau explains why a "legislator" might be necessary to convert a "multitude" into a civil society:

Of itself the people wills always the good, but of itself it by no means always sees it. The general will is always in the right, but the judgment which guides it is not always enlightened. It must be got to see objects as they are, and sometimes as they ought to appear to it. . . . The individuals see the good they reject; the public wills the good it does not see. All stand equally in need of guidance.

Behind both these passages stands a distinction most familiar to modern readers from Hobbes, between a "people" and a "multitude." As we now understand, following the work of Bruno Bernardi and Mike Sonenscher, the term *volonté générale* came into Rousseau from the 1706 Barbeyrac translation of Pufendorf's *De Iure Naturae*.[61] At VII.5.5, where Pufendorf was discussing the nature of democratic sovereignty in explicitly Hobbesian terms, he said that "in moral Considerations there is no manner of Absurdity in supposing, that those particular Wills [*volontez particulières*], which unite and conspire to make up the Will of the Community [*Corps Moral*], should want some Power or Quality which the general Will [*volonté générale*] is possess'd of."[62] He also said, "it requires no Depth of Parts to apprehend the Difference between all in general, and each in particular; between the Assembly of the People in Democracies, and private Men dispers'd according to their respective Habitations." The will of "private Men dispers'd" is what Rousseau termed in this passage "the will of all," and the "general will" is the will of the assembly as a single body.

We should not be too fixated on this terminology: Rousseau, followed by his early readers, was quite prepared to use the phrase "will of all" as a synonym for "general will": thus in the *Letters Written from the Mountain* (Letter 6) where he was summarizing *The Social Contract*, he stated that "The will of all is thus the order, the supreme rule, and that general and personified rule is what I call the Sovereign."[63] The reason for this looseness is that—as the famous remark about taking away the pluses and minuses illustrates—the general will *is* the will of all, with an appropriate mathematical transformation performed on it. The transformation is most easily understood as a rather elaborate description of calculating where the majority opinion is to be found; for example, if 100 people vote "yes" on a measure and 90 vote "no," the 90 "no" votes are "cancelled" by 90 "yes" votes, leaving 10 "yes" votes to determine the general will. He said something similar in *Poland*: "[T]he law, which is only the expression of the general will, is properly a resultant of all the particular interests combined and balanced in proportion to their number."[64] There is no suggestion in these passages that the building blocks (so to speak) of the general will are anything other than particular wills and private interests; the generality comes, as it did (for example) in Hobbes on democracy, from each citizen's willingness to make the majority will of the society his own, once the vote has taken place.[65]

The discrepancy that Rousseau feared between the general will and the "deliberations of the people" that might be corrupted in some way is explained in all these passages not by the ignorance or poor judgment of the individual citizens but (once a civil society has come into being) by the existence of *partial association*. The paragraph that immediately follows the famous passage in book II chapter 3 makes this absolutely clear. It reads:

> If, when the people, being furnished with adequate information, held its deliberations, the citizens had no communication one with another, the grand total of the small differences would always give the general will, and the decision would always be good. But when factions arise, and partial associations are formed

at the expense of the great association, the will of each of these associations becomes general in relation to its members, while it remains particular in relation to the State: it may then be said that there are no longer as many votes as there are men, but only as many as there are associations. The differences become less numerous and give a less general result. Lastly, when one of these associations is so great as to prevail over all the rest, the result is no longer a sum of small differences, but a single difference; in this case there is no longer a general will, and the opinion which prevails is purely particular.

This reminds us that Rousseau was as hostile to *deliberation*, and as scared of the power of orators, as Hobbes—his plea that citizens should have "no communication one with another" is what, I think, Sieyès was attacking in the remarks I quoted earlier ridiculing the democrats who fixed their individual opinions "in the watches of the night, with everyone in their own houses." There can be no disputing that it is only this aggregation of individual interests into partial associations that Rousseau believed to be the means by which the general will might be prevented from emerging from a vote. He said exactly the same after the equivalent passage in *Poland*:

> [T]he law, which is only the expression of the general will, is properly a resultant of all the particular interests combined and balanced in proportion to their number; but corporate interests, because of their too great weight, would upset the balance, and ought not, in their collective capacity, to be included in it. Each individual should have a vote; no corporate group of any kind should have one.[66]

As for the legislator, there is a well-known problem in all these kinds of social contract theories about how a disunited "multitude" can be turned into a "people," and Rousseau was clearly drawing, inter alia, on Cicero's account in the *De Inventione* I.2 of how men "scattered in the fields and hidden in sylvan retreats" could be fashioned by "a man—great and wise I am sure" into a single people. The essence of a "multitude" was that its members' wills were not *united*, *union* (as in Hobbes) being the subordination of their own wills to that of the majority, and without this commitment there could be no effective or stable general will. Rousseau solved the Hobbesian problem of how to get men in a state of nature to agree to agree (so to speak) by positing a legislator of the Ciceronian kind. But we should always remember that the legislator has no actual political *authority*:

> He . . . who draws up the laws has, or should have, no right of legislation, and the people cannot, even if it wishes, deprive itself of this incommunicable right, because, according to the fundamental compact, only the general will can bind the individuals, and there can be no assurance that a particular will is in conformity with the general will, until it has been put to the free vote of the people. (*Social Contract* III.7)

The epistemic democrats (to turn to them) can agree with all this, however, and still deny that Rousseau's general will is *in itself* the source of legitimacy in the state. This is because for them also, partial associations corrupt the general will, since the general will arises from the unconstrained expression of opinion about a political question by a very large number of independent voters. These interpreters of Rousseau instead lean heavily on some passages in book IV of *The Social Contract*, in particular one in chapter 2:

> When in the popular assembly a law is proposed, what the people is asked is not exactly whether it approves or rejects the proposal, but whether it is in conformity with the general will, which is their will. Each man, in giving his vote, states his opinion on that point; and the general will is found by counting votes. When therefore the opinion that is contrary to my own prevails, this proves neither more nor less than that I was mistaken, and that what I thought to be the general will was not so. If my particular opinion had carried the day I should have achieved the opposite of what was my will; and it is in that case that I should not have been free.

To this can be added a remark in book IV chapter 1, where Rousseau says of a man who sells his vote that

> [H]e does not extinguish in himself the general will, but only eludes it. The fault he commits is that of changing the state of the

question, and answering something different from what he is asked. Instead of saying, by his vote, "It is to the advantage of the State," he says, "It is of advantage to this or that man or party that this or that view should prevail."

It is easy to see why these look like epistemic arguments. But one must be careful. Rousseau nowhere says that the point of gathering "opinions" about the general will is to arrive at the right answer to a political problem, and in the climactic passage of *Letters Written from the Mountain* in which he appealed to the citizens of Geneva, he said expressly that this was *not* his idea.

> [A]bove all come together. You are ruined without resource if you remain divided. And why would you be divided when such great common interests unite you? . . . In a word, it is less a question of deliberation here than of concord; the choice of which course you will take is not the greatest question: Were it bad in itself, take it all together; by that alone it will become the best, and you will always do what needs to be done provided that you do so in concert.[67]

"Were it bad in itself, take it all together; by that alone it will become the best" is the key to Rousseau's thought: the generality of the general will *makes* it the right answer, it does not *detect* it. Rousseau did not believe that the correct course of action for a republic of his kind could be independently specified—only after the vote would such a thing come into existence. What mattered was the capacity of citizens to act together without dissension at the point of action, even if there had been great dissension before the final decision was made; and union after the decision had been taken required a general acceptance of the vote as the deciding factor, and the acceptance by the minority that they would commit themselves to what the majority wished to do.

In the first of these "epistemic" passages, Rousseau was, I think, in fact concerned primarily with the problem of why an individual should subordinate his will to that of the majority, as in Richard Wollheim's old "paradox."[68] The quotation from chapter 2 is explicitly an answer to the question of "how a man can be both free and forced to conform to wills that are not his own. How are the opponents at once free and subject to laws they have not agreed to?" And when he said that people are not exactly asked whether they approve or reject a measure, I think that he was saying what the level-headed responses to Wollheim, such as Ross Harrison's, said: that is, what you are asked is what your *provisional* view is, but not what in the final analysis you will be committed to, since that will only be known when the general will is ascertained.[69] It is an "opinion" in the sense that it is provisional and revisionable.

Importantly, this is perfectly compatible with it being the case that people vote in their own interests, as Rousseau frequently said, for example, in the passage from *Poland* quoted earlier—the law is "a resultant of all the particular interests combined and balanced in proportion to their number." I am not required to think about the common good when I decide what to vote for, since my commitment to the common good is satisfied simply by my willingness to subordinate my interest to that of the majority of my fellow citizens. The ballot tells us where the majority interest lies precisely *because* we have each followed our private interest in our vote. This does not preclude our having wishes for the collectivity and voting accordingly, but equally it does not preclude our voting in our own interests on straightforward matters of personal concern such as tax proposals. The key thing is that when we lose, we make the policy supported by our fellow citizens genuinely our own.[70]

The second of the two epistemic passages, about the vote seller, is slightly different. It occurs in the context of a further discussion of the danger of partial association, and the point that Rousseau seems to be making is that if I choose to belong to a partial association with coordinated voting (this, after all, is what a man who sells his vote agrees to) then I have ipso facto lost interest in the general will and am treating the voting process as a means to a partial victory. Again, this is different from a requirement on me *when I vote as an individual and not as a member of an association* not to vote in my own interests; indeed, precisely what is wrong with partial associations (in Rousseau's eyes) is that they commit me to subordinating my own interest to the interest of the group (or, if I simply sell my vote to one other person, to the interest of that person).

If what I have been saying so far is correct, then Rousseau was much more like Hobbes than many people have supposed. In particular, he resembled Hobbes in believing that laws, the acts of a sovereign, are inherently and inescapably *arbitrary*, and acquire their authority *only* from the fact that they are the will of the sovereign; though Rousseau (as I argued in *The Sleeping Sovereign*) believed that Hobbes had made a major error in supposing that the initial democracy he described in *De Cive* could turn itself into a despotism. Rousseau's early readers immediately saw the resemblance between the two of them in this respect. For example, Rousseau's erstwhile ally but now opponent, the Genevan pastor Jacob Vernet said, very perceptively:

> [B]elieving with *Hobbes* that men are born the enemies of one another, and that our worst enemies are our superiors, like him he remedies this by Despotism, though locating it in a different place. Whereas Hobbes gives arbitrary power to a Prince, Mr Rousseau (who knows no middle ground) instead gives a similar power to the multitude.[71]

This was a reference to the celebrated letter that Rousseau had written on 26 July of the previous year to Mirabeau; the letter was published in Mirabeau's *Précis de l'Ordre Légal* of 1768 and thereafter reprinted and noted regularly; it was included in Rousseau's *Oeuvres* of 1782 and in subsequent editions. Rousseau was responding to the gift by Mirabeau on behalf of its author of a copy of Mercier de La Rivière's recently published *L'Ordre Naturel et Essentiel des Sociétés Politiques*, one of the principal works of physiocracy, in which Mercier extolled "the empire of evidence" as the basis for law and called for an enlightened despotism that would legislate using evidence.[72] In the letter, Rousseau confessed,

> Here, according to my old ideas, is the great problem of Politics, which I compare to that of squaring the circle in Geometry, and of longitudes in Astronomy: *To find a form of Government that might place the law above man.*
>
> If this form can be found, let us look for it and try to establish it. You claim, Gentlemen, to find this dominant law in other people's evidence. You prove too much: for this evidence had to be in all Governments, or it will never be in a single one of them.

If unfortunately this form cannot be found, and I frankly admit that I believe that it cannot be, then I am of the opinion that one has to go to the other extreme and all at once place man as much above the law as he can be, consequently to establish a despotism that is arbitrary and indeed the most arbitrary possible: I would wish the despot could be God. In a word, I see no mean between the most austere Democracy and the most perfect Hobbesism: for the conflict between men and the laws, which makes for a perpetual intestine war in the State, is the worst of all political States.[73]

These remarks have often been misunderstood. We should take seriously Rousseau's comparison of the physiocratic ambition to "put laws above man" to squaring the circle or finding longitudes. By 1767 it was generally accepted that squaring the circle was indeed *impossible*, not just very difficult or not yet achieved (though a full proof had to wait another hundred years). It was also believed in the highest academic circles in France that clocks could not be used accurately to determine longitude, and that the problem might in practice remain insoluble.[74] So Rousseau was not saying that *faute de mieux*, one has to move to arbitrariness (with the implication, often drawn by his modern readers, that *mieux* might still be possible): he was saying that anything else is as impossible as squaring the circle, and that hoping to find some way of doing it will instead lead to "a perpetual intestine war in the State"—his overriding anxiety, which found expression in his plea to the citizens of Geneva to "take it all together; by that alone it will become the best." But of course, this was also Hobbes's overriding anxiety. "Hobbesism," for Rousseau in this context, simply meant a single sovereign of the Hobbesian kind, and "the most austere democracy" a democratic sovereign of the same kind: nothing else was possible, and a single sovereign was a form of tyranny; as he went on to say, "But the Caligulas, the Neros, the Tiberiuses! . . . My God! . . . I writhe on the ground, and bewail being a human being."

In his *Considerations* on Poland, Rousseau used the same analogy.

The subjecting of man to law is a problem in politics which I liken to that of the squaring of the circle in geometry. Solve this problem well, and the government based on your solution will be good and free from abuses. But until then you may rest assured that, wherever you think you are establishing the rule of law, it is men who will do the ruling.

There will never be a good and solid constitution unless the law reigns over the hearts of the citizens.[75]

And again, I think we are entitled to think that Rousseau believed it to be *impossible*, however desirable, to have a government in which men were subjected to law. Only if the citizens thought of the law as *theirs*, and the outcome solely of their wills, would the danger he described in the letter to Mirabeau be avoided, and much of the *Considerations* is, of course, devoted to suggestions about how citizens can come to think of themselves as actively engaged in a common project of law making rather than passively receiving laws handed down from some external authority.

In Rousseau, I would say, we have the first and possibly the greatest theorist of the kind of radical democracy that was espoused by those in the nineteenth century who were profoundly opposed to the modern post-revolutionary state. We should not try to domesticate him into our own liberal attitudes: his contemporaries who feared him were (by their own lights) right to do so, just as an earlier generation had been right to fear Hobbes, and a later generation was right to fear Marx. But the people who expressed these fears at least understood what it was they were fearing: the advent of a democracy with universal suffrage, in which all the conditions of political and economic life would in the last analysis be decided by a democratic process. Formally speaking, after two centuries of struggle, the states we now live in are, in fact, mostly committed to something like this picture (with some exceptions, such as Germany and India, whose constitutions include provisions that cannot be changed by popular vote). But in practice, they are quite far removed from it.

First, as we have seen, for these radical democrats there should be no distinction between *citizen* and *resident*: everyone engaged in the task of constructing a common life had to be able to vote on the conditions of their life together. Very few modern states now allow this, though the United States did so at least in its early years. I shall say more about this in my second chapter, as it is a useful corrective to the idea that we all have universal suffrage, even in theory. In practice, of course, many states are also very far removed from universal suffrage, through devices such as the denial of the vote to former felons, elaborate and difficult methods of registration, and cynical gerrymandering of districts. These failings are not restricted to the United States. Second, modern states have made it increasingly necessary for laws to meet rather general conditions imposed upon them by entrenched sets of rights that offer a great deal of scope for judicial interpretation and are very hard to alter, to the extent that (as we all know) presidential elections in the United States turn to an astonishing degree on what kind of people will next be appointed to the Supreme Court. Attempts to change this (including the remarkable proposal by Theodore Roosevelt that there should be a national plebiscite on any controversial judgment of the Supreme Court)[76] have always failed, and I find it hard to believe that there will be another amendment to the US Constitution in my lifetime. "Popular constitutionalism," of the kind championed by Larry Kramer, would (if it could be implemented) meet many of these objections; even Bentham was not opposed to constitutions and bodies of rights as long as they were essentially treated as ordinary legislation. There are many cultural forces pushing back against such an idea, however, and it would (I think) require the adoption (or re-adoption) of a genuinely democratic spirit across the whole of our politics in order for it to be achieved.

Why did that spirit disappear? There are many reasons, but chief among them I would put the disappearance of a mass labor force that between 1850 and 1950 produced the material conditions of a common life and then went to war to preserve it; the richest and most powerful people in society recognized that they (sometimes literally) owed their lives to the efforts of the poorest. The great advances in democratic institutions in the twentieth century, unsurprisingly, took place after the wars of the citizen armies (I would include in this the civil rights legislation of the 1960s, driven in part by the recognition that the United States could not continue segregation after the war). But the production of what we needed by the mass of our fellow citizens even in peacetime contributed to the sense of mutual dependence. But this has now gone and, with it, a widespread sense that we *need* all of our fellow citizens; instead, the rhetoric of many modern democrats is that we have to *help* them, and charity is not a strong enough principle to sustain genuine democracy; apart from anything else, as a long tradition from the ancient world to the eighteenth century recognized, the recipients of charity can come to hate their benefactors, since the acts of benevolence merely reveal ever more clearly the power differential between the people concerned.[77] But our fellow citizens are still there, and their capacity, if they choose and if they are permitted, to transform our lives through their actions is still there, and in my next chapter I propose to outline a modern version of the Rousseauian theory (as I have described it) that vindicates this.

2

Active Democracy

I

I want to begin this chapter by reminding you of what I said in my first one. In it, I drew a distinction between what I think are the two most powerful theories of a modern state. The first I associated with the Abbé Sieyès, though also with Constant and Hegel. On this account, the key features of the state are, first, that it protects the fundamental rights of all its residents, and second, that it has an institutional structure designed to represent the interests of the residents in the process of political decision-making, without putting direct control in their hands. As I said, it is no coincidence that Sieyès in the course of his theorizing should have distinguished between "active" and "passive" citizens; *activity*, from a Sieyèsian perspective, is not a particularly salient feature of politics, and indeed might endanger the structures set up to provide protection for rights and the responsible discussion of political questions. Modern theorists of a Sieyèsian sort will not go as far as he did in resisting (or, as I showed, in fact *abolishing*) universal suffrage, but the vote in practice means almost as little to them as it did to Sieyès, since it is hemmed in by all sorts of limitation on what it can achieve. And many of them are quite prepared to leave in place a distinction between "active" citizen and "passive" resident alien, one of Sieyès's two principal examples of "passivity"; the other, of course, being women.

The second theory I associated with Rousseau, but also with Bentham and Marx and the tradition of radical democracy in the nineteenth century exemplified by the Paris Commune. The central convictions of writers and activists in this tradition have been, first, that if I have not played a part in legislating, laws have no authority over me (I shall turn to what "playing a part" might mean later); and second, that democracy is best understood as a means of collective *action*, giving human beings the capacity radically to transform the conditions of their life. On this view, the essential characteristic of democratic politics is that the citizens are aware of themselves as engaged in constructing this common activity, and are willing to allow the wishes of a majority to override their own wishes, and their (possibly quite correct) belief that the majority of their fellow citizens are wrong. As Rousseau said in his striking remark at the end of *Letters Written from the Mountain*, which I quoted in the first chapter, "it is less a question of deliberation here than of concord; the choice of which course you will take is not the greatest question: Were it bad in itself, take it all together; by that alone it will become the best."

This theory plainly implies universal suffrage, that is, suffrage for anyone whose daily life is under the authority of the state (i.e., anyone other than the most temporary visitor), and we duly find this being argued for by most of these theorists—even Rousseau, I claimed, should be read in a generous fashion to include among his *citoyens* both resident aliens and (I recognize more controversially) women. Indeed, I think that universal suffrage was in practice a touchstone for this attitude to the modern state, and the slowness of the extension of the franchise in almost all countries from the 1830s to the 1940s is testimony not so much to the difficulty of changing social prejudices (though clearly that was part of it) as to the force of a quite modern idea about the state, of a broadly Sieyèsian kind, which as I said made universal suffrage unnecessary or undesirable. The shift in attitudes to the suffrage between Bentham and John Stuart Mill is an illustration of this—Bentham's confidence was replaced by Mill's caution, not because Mill was clinging to pre-Benthamite prejudices, but because he was much more open than Bentham had been to ideas of a Sieyèsian type, as we see in his admiration for Tocqueville.

II

What I want to do in this chapter is to defend a theory of this Rousseauian kind against its modern critics, and against the idea that *representation* of some kind is or should be the essence of democracy. The best way to bring out its distinctive features, I think, is to compare it with a set of theories of democracy that have been popular for some time with professional philosophers and are increasingly becoming popular with political activists, ideas that can be classified under the general heading of theories of *sortition*. Their fundamental characteristic is the idea that a lottery of some kind should be used in many instances where we would otherwise use voting; their advocates tend to call in aid the practices of ancient Athens, where sortition was treated as a natural feature of a democracy. Aristotle, in fact, observed that "the appointment of magistrates by lot is thought to be democratical, and the election of them oligarchical" (*Politics* IV.9). It should be said that while sortition was indeed used extensively at Athens in choosing officials, it was always alongside majority voting on other matters, including legislation.[1] It should also be said that it was not used at Rome, though Rome was much closer in character to our mass democracies. At Rome, sortition was only used (as it is in our societies) to choose juries: otherwise everything was decided by majority voting, though often of a complex kind. We still live, more or less, in political societies of the Roman and not the Athenian type, and the oldest of our institutions to use majority voting to make decisions, the Catholic Church, traces its institutional origins straightforwardly back to its beginnings in Rome.[2] Rousseau, as is well known, was profoundly interested in the politics of Rome and in its various voting methods, but was rather contemptuous of Athens, which he described as not a democracy but an aristocracy of orators.[3]

One of the most thorough discussions of sortition as an alternative to election has been in the work of Alexander Guerrero.[4] He has argued that a lottery would be a better means of choosing the members of a legislature than a vote, since it would respect more than voting does the essential principle of *equality* among the citizens. This is so (according to Guerrero) not merely because of the formal respect in which elections do not cleave closely to the principle of equality—that is, the simple fact that not all citizens can be candidates—but also because a lottery might substantively render politics more equal, since it would not be vulnerable to the manipulation by social power and wealth that is such a familiar feature of elections. The idea that a *legislature* might be chosen by lot is, of course, a radical one, but a

preference for lotteries over elections is to be found also in the growing enthusiasm for citizen juries to play a role in policymaking. There
are two aspects to a citizen jury: one is that it listens to the arguments
of experts on various aspects of the question presented to it in an
organized fashion, but this can also be a feature of an elected assembly (committees in Parliament and Congress regularly do this, after
all). The more distinctive feature is that the jury, like a jury in a criminal trial, is chosen by lot, and it is this that (in the eyes of the advocates for citizen juries) gives the institution its special character.

The point of a lottery, however, is not merely to preserve the
principle of democratic equality: implicit in it (and often explicit) is
the idea that it can be more *representative* of the population, in the
sense that its composition can mirror the composition of the entire
society with regard to what can be thought of as its relevant characteristics, such as wealth or ethnic identity. Two notions of representation coexist uneasily in modern political thought, as my friend and
colleague at Harvard Eric Nelson has recently observed in a brilliant
piece of historical reconstruction.[5] One is the idea that we should
choose people to represent us in an assembly where we cannot ourselves be present. We might want to give these representatives carte
blanche to do what they think best, or we might want to keep them
under our own control; this is the most obvious difference between
Sieyès and Rousseau. But the other notion of representation, which
is very prominent today but was also familiar during the nineteenth
century, is that the assembly should *mirror* the population.[6] In this
picture, the fact that the representatives are chosen by the electorate,
though possibly desirable, is less significant than their possession of
an appropriate social character, and may indeed conflict with it
(hence all-women shortlists now, or what amounted to all working-
class shortlists with the rise of the Labour Party a century ago). The
mirror picture has little or nothing in common with the Rousseauian
idea,[7] but it does overlap with the Sieyèsian one, since on the Sieyèsian
account the fact of choice is also really secondary to the characteristics of the representatives—as Sieyès himself acknowledged, election
might be a practical necessity in a modern state, but he thought that
it should be severely circumscribed in its effects. The revival of sortition has brought out the difference between these two kinds of

representation very vividly, since a system of sortition is intensely concerned with mirroring but has abandoned electoral choice.

Because of this feature, a citizen jury has at the very least to be a large number of people: the principle of equality would be preserved, strictly speaking, by a lottery that produced a single person, but no one thinks that such a system would be democratic if the random dictator were to be given any political power. (A friend of mine once suggested that the queen of England should be replaced by a citizen chosen annually by lot, but not even Guerrero has supposed that the president of the United States could be chosen in such a way). A very large number of people chosen entirely at random might succeed in being representative, but most advocates of citizen juries have usually supposed that something like the techniques of modern opinion polling should be used to put the jury together. These techniques, in fact, depend on mirroring the population: they do not nowadays consist merely of randomly sampling the entire population but instead use a careful selection of relevant characteristics to put together a sample that will adequately represent the population. On the whole, these techniques have proved remarkably successful, and one interesting reason for the resurgence of sortition might be the availability of sophisticated polling, something unknown until the mid-twentieth century. But even in antiquity it was assumed that a lottery for magistrates should be designed to have some representational character of this kind—Aristotle (again) said that "it is . . . a good plan that those who deliberate should be elected by vote or by lot in equal numbers out of the different classes" (*Politics* IV.14), which looks like an attempt to make sure that class divisions were represented in the deliberative body.

The fact that modern polling techniques would be needed to construct an appropriate jury also points to the possibility that one could select policies *simply* on the basis of polling, without the additional element of a jury sitting to hear evidence. The two features are separable, and it would be perfectly feasible for an advocate of sortition to argue that if it is true that opinion polling works as a means of representing the views of a population, then we should treat it as at least as authoritative as the result of a plebiscite or general election— and indeed as more authoritative, in that it would not have been corrupted by an electoral process. The fact that we do not, and that there is an important distinction in most people's minds between a "mere" opinion poll and an actual vote, is, I think, a good illustration of the central problem of sortition as the vehicle for democratic politics, and I shall return to this point presently.

There is another quite fashionable democratic theory that has an affinity with sortition, though it has normally been treated as different from it. This is the "epistemic" theory, which I discussed in my first chapter in the context of the interpretation of Rousseau. On the face of it, the epistemic theory is committed to majority voting and not to sortition, but in reality it is only an ersatz form of majoritarianism. This is first and most obviously because the authority of the decision rests not on the fact that the majority voted for it but on the fact it is the right course of action, and the vote is merely evidence for that, and conceivably not the only or the best kind of evidence. But equally important is the fact that, as I said in my first chapter, *universality* is not at all a necessary aspect of an epistemic theory. *Equality* is, since a vital aspect of the epistemic theory is that the participants all have an equal chance of answering the question correctly, but a suitable lottery of voters would work just as well at securing the epistemic result as universal suffrage and, indeed, in most circumstances would work much better. So the epistemic theory is in its essence quite close to the idea of sortition, since each theory is interested in reaching a political decision through a process in which people are given an equal chance of something—either an equal chance of participating in legislation, or an equal chance of arriving at the right answer to a political question. It is not an accident that the epistemic theory has its roots in Condorcet's theory not of an electorate, but of a *jury*.

Sortition is a particularly clear-cut alternative to a Rousseauian theory since it is an unusually pure example of what we might call representation without agency. It has revived because Sieyèsian representation has come to seem unrealistic—modern assemblies do not consist of wise and responsible individuals deliberating judiciously over the future of their country, but of hacks and placemen, put into the assembly through the power of money or the power of a party. But the turn to sortition has patently been a turn away from electoral democracy *as such*, and by playing down the significance of the vote, it leaves the mass of citizens with no *active* role at all; each one *passively* awaits the result of the lottery, in the hope (or maybe the fear) of being called to participate in law making. It is the purest version of representation, in which there is no agency on the part of the citizens at all, and in this respect it corresponds to, but goes even further than, the other constraints on the vote, such as entrenched constitutions which, as I said in my first chapter, have been characteristic of modern politics since the 1790s.

III

There are two principal reasons why a contempt for modern electoral politics has led people right back to sortition and not back simply to the eighteenth and nineteenth centuries' traditions of plebiscites and mandation. One is a general fear of mass political action and the consequences of strong majoritarianism, a fear I will return to later. The other reason is deeper and more theoretically interesting: it is a belief that the central idea in an active or agentive view of politics, that when I vote I am actually *effecting* something, is simply false. From the 1950s onwards, political scientists took it for granted that an individual's vote, or any other contribution to a large-scale enterprise, is extremely unlikely to make any difference to the outcome. The classic illustration of this is the so-called pivotal voter theory, according to which a rational agent would only vote for instrumental reasons if the chances of their being "pivotal"—that is, it is their vote which turns the election—were reasonably high.

Implicit in the pivotal voter theory is the assumption that I would vote for the same sort of reason that I would hand over money in a market, that is, that without doing so I would not receive the good I am paying for. And indeed an analogy between an election and a market has been quite pervasive in the modern literature, beginning with Mises in the 1932 edition of his book *Socialism: An Economic and Sociological Analysis*.

When we call a capitalist society a consumers' democracy we mean that the power to dispose of the means of production, which belongs to the entrepreneurs and capitalists, can only be acquired by means of the consumers' ballot, held daily in the market-place. Every child who prefers one toy to another puts its voting paper in the ballot-box, which eventually decides who shall be elected captain of industry.[8]

Mises even drew an explicit comparison between Mill's plural votes and the extra leverage that wealth gives in this "electoral" process. The same rough analogy between voting and a market has been drawn by various other people, including Kenneth Arrow and, above all, Anthony Downs. For most people other than Mises, it should be said, it is only an *analogy*; they recognize that in an election, the voter is voting with a deliberate and express intention to bring about a *collective* outcome, and the vote is merely the means to do this. As I wrote in my first chapter, this is not the same as saying that the voter is thinking about the common good in a *disinterested* fashion. He may support a certain kind of outcome for purely self-interested reasons, but it is still a collective outcome that he has in view. In a market, however, this is evidently not the case—Mises's child would be astonished to be told that it was voting for a captain of industry rather than choosing the toy it wanted. Nevertheless, the idea that a vote operates rather like money in a market is quite widespread at a popular level, and it has led to a strange distortion of people's attitudes to voting; in the aftermath of Trump's election, I heard an interview on NPR with a protester against the new president, who said in tones of outrage "I didn't vote for *this*"—as if Amazon had failed to deliver the goods they had ordered.

Since in normal elections no one is likely to be a pivotal voter, most modern theorists of democracy have supposed that, if they are acting rationally, voters must intend something else by voting than actually to bring about a desired outcome. The most favored candidate for their intention is that they are *expressing* themselves; what is striking about this explanation, however, is that it either puts the act of voting into the same category as other kinds of self-expression, such as carrying banners and the like, or treats it as a kind of private smugness; either way, it downgrades the distinctive character of the *vote*. The voter, on a Rousseauian account, believes that he is involved in making a collective *decision* when he votes, but an expressive account disregards the distinctively decisive character of the vote; it has to, after all, since it denies that in normal circumstances any one vote *can* be decisive. It is perfectly possible, for example, to engage in all these expressive acts in a state where decisions are made through sortition: I may wish to influence the citizen jury or the experts who testify before it, but I will not be one of the group which finally makes the decision. An unwillingness to take votes entirely seriously, manifested in this country by the recent tendency of state legislatures to undermine or ignore popular plebiscites,[9] and in Britain (of course) by the struggle over Brexit, may be a consequence of thinking of them as expressive, since it treats them as just another kind of evidence about popular opinion, to be balanced against other considerations rather than being accorded the decisiveness with which traditional democratic theory viewed them.

Another candidate is that the voters are acting out of a sense of fairness—they do not want other citizens to go through the effort of voting while they stay at home enjoying the benefits of the process (either the victory of their side, or the general benefits of a stable political system). The problem with this interpretation is that fairness is—so to speak—a secondary quality. If a system of collective action is in place, it might well be true that I ought to contribute to it. But fairness cannot be an explanation of why the system was chosen in the first place: I can be perfectly fair towards my fellows citizens under a regime of sortition, or indeed under any method of making political decisions. There has to be some point to the choice of a *voting* system, and some motivation for people to vote, other than the principle of a just distribution of burdens. And for a Rousseauian, that point is the fact that I am self-legislating: when I take part in the vote, I am actually contributing to the formation of the laws I live under.

Some years I ago I published a book[10] in which I explored the assumptions behind the idea that only a pivotal voter can think of themself as bringing about an outcome. What I argued there was that the implicit assumption in this account of voting is that the only situation in which I have an instrumental reason for voting is one where my vote is *necessary* to achieve the outcome I desire. But in fact, it is also possible for me to have an instrumental reason if my vote is *sufficient*, though in that situation I have to have the further or "meta" desire that it should be I who is bringing about the result. This sounds subtle and complex, but it can be understood fairly easily through the example of a serial vote, in which one after another we step up to vote for one of two candidates or legislative measures. At some point there will be a majority for one of the options, and we can imagine that we stop counting the votes at that point (Roman elections were rather like this). The last voter's vote decided the election, and so (we can say) he certainly had an instrumental reason for casting his ballot. By the same token, all the earlier voters who cast their ballots for the winning candidate can pride themselves on equally contributing to the outcome—each vote was decisive, conditional upon the other votes being cast. However, suppose that there were still a lot of voters in line waiting to vote when the ballot was stopped. Many of them *would have* voted for the winning candidate, so if the last voter had not bothered to turn up, the result would have been the same. His vote was not pivotal, in the sense of being necessary to secure the outcome, but it was sufficient. And if he wanted to be someone who actually made a difference to the result, he could do so by voting; though if he did *not* want to be that kind of person, he had no particular reason to vote even though he wanted the outcome of the ballot. In other words, he could choose to be an agent and act in order to secure his goal, or he could choose merely to be a passive recipient of it.

Serial voting of the kind I have imagined is now very rare in practice, but in premodern voting systems it was quite common. Any election that takes the form of an assembly in which people step up to register their vote in public will have this character, and that was the shape elections took in both England and France before the coming of the secret ballot in the late nineteenth century.[11] But the underlying logic is still the same in modern systems, and indeed it can be quite vividly experienced in the British system. Many of us have watched the count in a constituency, and seen the paper ballots piling up for each candidate. At some point in the evening, it can become clear that enough ballots for one of them have been counted to guarantee that that candidate has won. If my ballot is in that pile, I can feel just like the voter in the serial vote—*my* piece of paper is part of the sufficient set of ballots. If it has not yet been counted, I will not be able to feel quite like that; but if I have voted for a winning candidate, the chance that my ballot is part of the sufficient or (what I will call) the "efficacious" set in a two-person race must by definition be more than 50 percent. This is a vivid example, but the same reasoning applies even in an American-style election with voting machines: if there are enough people who vote like me, I can think of myself as having a high probability of contributing effectively to an electoral outcome, and certainly a probability high enough to make it worth my while to vote, given my desire to play a real and effective part in the process.

This is the point that has largely been overlooked in the modern theory of voting, and it is the key reason why in the end there can be no real analogy between market behavior and voting. In a market, there is no point in my handing over money if I am going to get the thing for free, whereas there could be an instrumental point in my voting even if someone else would step up in my place and secure the election of my candidate. It might be a matter of great importance to me in a political context that it was *I* who brought about the result. There is, of course, an element of what might be thought of as expressiveness in this, in that I am motivated by the value to me of the action; but it is only of value to me *because* it is instrumental, and because I can rightly think I am achieving something directly through my vote.

There is a question that in its general form has not received as much attention as it deserves: in what circumstances do I want to bring about a result myself, even if someone else is morally certain to bring it about if I do not? For most economists, my desire to do something myself is merely an extra desire added to the wish to possess a particular good and can be treated simply as a matter of personal taste—some people (including me) like DIY, some don't. But there are areas where this looks implausible; the one that has received philosophical attention is charity or altruism, where it seems odd to say that I passionately want the hungry to be fed, but I would rather someone else did it.[12] I think myself that it is a fundamental feature of human existence that we *do* things: there is something very alien about the idea of a way of life in which we simply receive goods without actively *getting* them.[13] But we do not need to go into that more general issue here, since our participation in democratic politics looks like a very good instance of something where my agency is critical. If Rousseau and the other radical democrats were right in saying that laws have no full authority over me—or, to put it another way, that the state is in some sense alien to me—unless I have taken part in making its collective decisions, then I cannot as a democrat look on my participation as being like a preference for making my own coffee table rather than buying one.

On an agentive view of this kind, majoritarianism will arise very naturally. On the one hand, if a vote required unanimity, then clearly there would be very few times that any collective action could actually be agreed upon. Each time it was, I would indeed have taken a full part in determining the result, but because there would be so few occasions on which we could do anything, my overall agency—my capacity to transform the world in some way—would not be very great. And on the other hand, if a minority regularly got its way, then by definition any particular member of the community would be likely to have less agency than if the decision was taken in accordance with the wishes of the majority.

This account seems to me to be more plausible than the most serious recent argument for majoritarianism, that put forward by Jeremy Waldron.[14] Waldron has argued that the attraction of majoritarianism is that it is a decision procedure that respects both the principle of equality and the principle that "the fact that a given member of the group holds a certain view" has "positive decisional weight." The latter principle can be rephrased as *all other things being equal,* one member can decide the matter, and each of us could be that member—it is not specified in advance who it should be. Waldron had to propose this rather odd principle because a few pages earlier he had assumed that a vote makes no difference to the outcome, has no "positive decisional weight," unless it is pivotal. There are two problems about his view, however. First, why should the mere possibility that a pivotal voter could decide an outcome be a reason for me to accept a majoritarian decision where there was *not* a majority of only one vote? But second, and I think more interesting, what would Waldron say about a well-organized process of sortition?[15] As we have seen, it certainly meets his fundamental test of equality among the citizens; a majoritarian form of sortition, as in a jury, also meets the condition of an equal chance of being pivotal. But it is, I think, not the kind of majoritarian democracy that Waldron wanted to defend.

Supermajorities, on the "active" account of democracy, are a matter of judgment (as indeed Rousseau said):[16] to require a supermajority is to render the proposed course of action less likely, but it does ensure that a larger group of people support the proposal. In general, however, there is a good reason to support a straight majority as a decision procedure, perhaps *especially* on important matters: a population that thinks that the status quo is unduly privileged, and that a minority of the population can block urgent change, may come to feel a general hostility to their political institutions. The experience of America with regard to its constitutional constraints, such the difficulty in overturning the *Citizens United* judgment, is not reassuring.

Political scientists have often been puzzled by the so-called bandwagon effect, but on this account it is entirely rational (given, as I said, my desire to take part) to join a bandwagon that corresponds more or less to what I want; this is the natural origin of political parties, which so many modern political theorists treat with a kind of high-minded disdain.[17] Furthermore, if my vote is a means of doing things and not merely a way of expressing a preference, it makes sense to think about *bargaining* with it, or forming coalitions with other voters who may want different things from me. Again, we must assume that I *want* to be effective in some way, and do not *need* to be; but with that caveat, I can think about different ways of being effective, and some of those ways may not simply be voting for what I want. If it is possible for us to think of our vote as having an effect, it must be possible for us to think strategically about it. So a stark contrast between getting what I want and failing to get it may be misleading; there will almost always be new possibilities for me to get some of what I want if I can ally in some way with enough of my fellow citizens.

IV

Moreover, any defeat is often likely to be temporary and provisional, a feature of democratic politics of the utmost importance; it is the temporary nature of any defeat that damps down the violent passions of the losers, since they live to fight again another day. Compare the politics of abortion in the United States and the United Kingdom; indeed, I might say (though I am of course *parti pris*) that the history of the United Kingdom, at least down to the 1970s, is an often overlooked vindication of rather pure majoritarianism. One might not have expected that the country with the least constraints on its legislature of any in the world should have had a (relatively) stable and tolerant history, but I would say that it is precisely *because* there were no constraints that it had this history. The passions unleashed by Brexit illustrate what happens when a tradition of this sort is broken, and one side thinks it can have a near-permanent victory by entrenching in the United Kingdom the kind of economic policies embodied in the EU treaties.

This possibility, that an unconstrained electorate might, counterintuively, be a more reliable basis for civil peace than a system of entrenched rights, should receive more attention from the defenders of what is often called "liberal" democracy than it does. It is, I believe, the same thought that Rousseau expressed in his letter to Mirabeau when he warned that an attempt to avoid arbitrary rule would merely lead to "the conflict between men and the laws, which makes for a perpetual intestine war in the State, [and] is the worst of all political States."[18] Resentment at the inaccessible sources of power represented by the constraints on an electorate can indeed lead to a "perpetual intestine war," as we have often seen in our own time.

Most clear cases of so-called illiberal democracy, in fact, involve taking the vote away from minorities, either formally, through denying them citizenship, or informally, through corruption of the voting process, and this is actually testimony to the fact that majoritarianism, as long as it respects the clear condition that every one should always have the vote, is not as potentially illiberal as people often imagine. In reality (as distinct from the abstract fears of antimajoritarians) a tyrannical majority can never be confident that coalitions of voters cannot be constructed to oppose them unless they deny the minority the vote. An obvious example is the way Reconstruction in the American South was brought to a halt, but even the Nazi war on Jews began with the Denaturalization Law of 1933 and the Citizenship Law of 1935.[19]

The possibility that a democracy might pass laws of this kind is, however, sometimes used as an argument against the principle of majoritarianism, but that is to miss the point. It is rather like the equally mistaken idea that a fundamental problem with the principle of toleration is that it entails tolerating the intolerant. If doing so destroys the possibility of living in accordance with the principle, most people recognize, then it does not follow that the intolerant should be tolerated. From the Rousseauian perspective, the fundamental criterion for the authority of law is the universality of its origin in the popular will, and a democracy that deprived some of its citizens of the vote would simply have ceased to be a democracy, and could claim no legitimacy for its acts. Its leaders would have staged a coup, and there would be no difference between this and a democracy simply handing over all its power to a single ruler. In his discussion of this process in book III chapter 10 of *The Social Contract*, Rousseau referred to it as *usurpation*. No known political system can in the end guard against coups; if the judges of the supreme court of a country with a completely entrenched constitution choose to interpret it in an illegitimate fashion, what recourse is left to the citizens? The most relevant question is, what kind of political system is least likely to engender the kind of hostilities that might lead to a coup? (Bearing in mind that political systems of any kind may not in the end be all that powerful against overwhelming social forces). And a perfectly plausible answer to this question is, a system that offers the maximum scope for a relatively rapid change of policy, such that no one feels permanently prevented from getting something of what they want politically.

V

Practical considerations of this kind have played an important part in the intuitive hostility many people feel to a Rousseauian account of democracy, but there is another, more theoretically salient doubt that is often expressed. It can be phrased as: in what sense is the result of a vote in which I have taken part *my action* if I have in fact been outvoted? The answer to this question that Rousseau and the other early theorists of democracy (including, in this respect, Hobbes) always gave was, it is my action if I have agreed beforehand that I will accept the result of a majority vote. As Rousseau said in book I chapter 5 of *The Social Contract,*

> if there were no prior convention, where, unless the election were unanimous, would be the obligation on the minority to submit to the choice of the majority? How have a hundred men who wish for a master the right to vote on behalf of ten who do not? The law of majority voting is itself something established by convention, and presupposes unanimity, on one occasion at least.

But there is a major problem with this way of putting the thought, and it comes out clearly through a comparison with Hobbes. Hobbes had said in *De Cive* (where he thought most deeply about democracy), like Rousseau, that

> if the move towards formation of a commonwealth is to get started, each member of a crowd [*multitudo*] must agree with the others that on any issue anyone brings forward in the group, the wish of the majority shall be taken as the will of all; for otherwise, a crowd will never have any will at all, since their attitudes and aspirations differ so markedly from one another. (VI.2)

Unlike Rousseau, however, he believed that this majoritarian democracy could pass its authority on to an aristocracy or monarchy, since he took the relationship of the individual citizen to the democratic assembly of which he was part to be the same as his relationship to a monarch. In each case, the citizen had agreed that whatever the assembly, or the monarch, should decide, the decision would count as his own will. On this view, the outvoted member of an assembly is no different from a citizen who takes no part in its proceedings, nor indeed from a citizen of a country where there is no democracy: anyone who is willing to abide by the constitutional structure has given this general authority to the sovereign to act on their behalf. But if this is the basis for saying that the action of a majority is "mine" even though I am outvoted, then by the same token, the action of the majority is "mine" even though I did not vote at all, and that seems to undermine completely the force of the Rousseauian thought that we must all take part in an active fashion in making our laws. All politics once again becomes representational.

But the way Rousseau himself phrased the point about prior unanimity made it (I think) too Hobbesian; what he had in mind was in reality closer to *posterior* unanimity than *prior* unanimity, with the necessary condition that I should first have taken part in the vote. The difference between the two comes out most clearly in what I called in my first chapter the most levelheaded responses to Richard Wollheim's so-called paradox, such as Ross Harrison's. What these responses pointed out is that my initial vote is *provisional*: as a democrat, I agree that once the majority view is known, I accept it as my own. This democratic commitment is indeed prior to the vote, as Rousseau thought, but the alignment of my will with the will of the majority (to use the Rousseauian language) is posterior: henceforward I will act on the basis of a belief that the correct course of action *for me* is to do what the majority of my fellow citizens have expressly voted for.[20]

One important implication of this was brought out by Condorcet in his *On the necessity of a ratification of the constitution by the citizens* of August 1789, in a passage that also confirms that this is the right way to interpret a Rousseauian position.

> Any law accepted by the plurality [*pluralité*] of the inhabitants of a nation can be taken as having unanimous support: given the need to accept or to reject the law and to follow the plurality opinion [*l'opinion du plus grand nombre*], anyone who rejects a proposed law will already have decided to abide by it if it is supported by the plurality. This kind of unanimous approval will continue for as long as those who were alive at the time continue to form a plurality, since they were all able to consent to live by this law for this length of time. But such approval becomes meaningless as soon as these individuals cease to form a plurality of the nation.
>
> Thus, the length of time for which any constitutional law [*loi constitutionnelle*] can remain in force is the time it takes for half of the citizens alive when the law was passed to be replaced by new ones. This is easily calculated, and takes about 20 years if the age of majority is fixed at 21, and 18 years if the age of majority is 25 [given a much lower life expectancy in eighteenth-century France than in the twenty-first-century United States or United Kingdom].

The same is true of constitutions that are produced by a Convention, because then, once again, the plurality (and by extension all) of the citizens agree to abide by this constitution.

I consider it very important to set a maximum period for which a law can remain irrevocable. People no longer dare claim that there can legitimately be perpetual laws.[21]

Thomas Jefferson said exactly the same as Condorcet in his well-known letters from Paris to James Madison and Richard Gem in 1789, concluding that nineteen years was the appropriate time to revisit the US Constitution. He had presumably just read Condorcet's pamphlet.[22]

On this view, the actual implementation of a vote by an assembly is unanimous; at the point at which (for example) the resolution of an assembly becomes a law, there *is* no minority. An important feature of this approach is that it avoids the theoretical—and indeed metaphysical—problems implicit in the idea of group agency as distinct from joint agency (to use the helpful distinction, e.g., in Pettit and List).[23] The assembly for Condorcet or Jefferson is simply a set of individuals each of whose wills have been aligned in the same direction at the point of final decision, and it does not have any strong corporate identity.

One reason this generation of democrats feared the notion of corporate identity was because, as Condorcet said, they feared the idea of perpetual laws. Or as Jefferson said, returning to the subject in 1816,

It is now forty years since the constitution of Virginia was formed. [The tables of mortality] inform us, that, within that period, two-thirds of the adults then living are dead. Have then the remaining third, even if they had the wish, the right to hold in obedience to their will, and to laws heretofore made by them, the other two-thirds, who, with themselves, compose the present mass of adults? If they have not, who has? The dead? But the dead have no rights. . . . This corporeal globe, and everything upon it, belongs to its present corporeal inhabitants, during their generation. They alone have a right to direct what is the concern of themselves alone, and to declare the law of that direction; and this direction can only be made by their majority.[24]

Remember what I wrote in my first chapter about Bentham's attack on Sieyès for his desire to govern France "for ages after we are no more."

They also feared perpetual, or at least prolonged, *debt*: their arguments applied not only to constitutional measures but also to public debt. On their account, a debt was contracted by the individuals acting in concert in the same fashion as it would have been by an individual acting alone, and it expired in the same way; the fact that (speaking metaphorically) an assembly might live for ever did not mean that its debts could continue in perpetuity. The practical point of their argument was, then, that no assembly could bind its successors for longer than twenty years—it could of course repeal normal laws within this time period, but if it asserted that the law had some special status and degree of permanence, like a constitution, it could not make it last longer than twenty years. The dream of permanent laws has somewhat receded (except in Germany), but public debt remains a good example of how a state can commit itself to an obligation that it cannot rescind at any time of its choosing. On Condorcet or Jefferson'a account, however, an assembly could not undertake a debt with an expiry date of more than twenty years.

If we apply Condorcet's reasoning to a modern state such as the United Kingdom, the time limit is about forty-two years,[25] which oddly enough is almost exactly the interval between the first EU referendum and the second! It is as if people possess an intuitive sense of when a major constitutional provision should be reopened. It is also the case that on the whole, governments do not nowadays borrow on a timescale of more than thirty years (i.e., the longest-term standard US Treasury bond is thirty years), just as many of us have mortgages for the same period. This was by no means true even in the recent past, and governments still issue some undated bonds.[26] But if we exclude such cases, we can in practice get many of the features for which we might suppose a strong theory of group identity was necessary, such as reliable public debts, without having to postulate anything more than what we might term Condorcet agency.

Though a view of this kind illustrates why we should not regard a majority in the assembly as *representing* the minority, since at the critical point of decision there is no longer a minority, a question still remains about the importance of taking part in the legislative process, rather than merely agreeing beforehand that the legislative process should represent one's will. Why does taking part in the final determination of the assembly carry more weight than giving the assembly a blanket authorization to act on my behalf, and why should Rousseau have been so emphatic that representation, at least at the fundamental level, was not enough to secure the legitimacy of the constitution?

To see what Rousseau, and democrats like him, might have had in mind, let us first think about the difference between a crowd of people with a clear common purpose (a mob heading towards the Bastille, let us say) and the bystanders cheering them on or quietly endorsing their project. The mob is about to *accomplish something*, to actually change the physical character of the world, in a way that the bystanders are not. The bystanders may be contributing causally to the action in some fashion—for example, by raising the adrenalin level of the members of the mob—but they are not *part* of the action. And if it is said that, equally, some members of the mob are not part of the action, despite their common purpose, remember what I argued earlier about participation in a vote. It is possible to say for each of the members that there is a reasonable chance that they are part of an efficacious set—in this case, the number of people needed to break the gates of the prison—and that this knowledge can spur them all into action. But the bystanders cannot be part of *any* efficacious set.

A parliamentary assembly, on this view of the matter, is like a mob; and in the case of the House of Commons, at least, its ancient physicality is emphasized by the smallness of the Chamber (too small, deliberately, for the number of members),[27] and by the lobbies into which MPs crowd to vote. An assembly's ability to transform the physical character of the world is of course not immediate but requires a complicated apparatus of bureaucrats, policemen, et cetera. But it is the location for the decisive action that sets all this apparatus in motion (as Churchill specifically said in the quotation in n. 27 above). And once the votes have been taken, the legislative act is (on the Condorcet view) the will of each member. So there is an action taking place there that is specific to those people in that place and involves each of them in the act of legislating.

One way of capturing what is implied in the agentive view is precisely that it takes democracy to be in effect a kind of civilized and domesticated version of a mob—and that should not alarm us. Human beings when they gather together physically can effect great changes; it is not an accident that the famous revolutionary moments are cases of mass action, such as the storming of the Bastille or the Winter Palace. And even in our own time, the major changes in world politics have been signalled by people actually meeting in large numbers and physically taking action, from the Paris streets in May 1968 through the Gdansk shipyard, the Berlin Wall, and Tiananmen Square to Maidan and Tahrir Square. Beneath our placid democratic procedures there is still this ancient fact. The great discovery of democracy was that people could accept a simple head count as the basis for the transformation that they might otherwise have effected through physical action and, potentially, violence.

VI

As I have already stressed, a Rousseauian view of democracy has as a natural implication universal suffrage, and in particular suffrage for *habitants, resident aliens.* Very few modern states now allow this, though in the United States, at least, it was widespread in the first thirty years or so of the new republic. As Jamie Raskin has observed, it was not until after 1812 that it began to be abandoned, though exceptions continued throughout the nineteenth century; it finally disappeared from all states and from all elections at any level in 1928. But it has never been declared unconstitutional, and in recent years a number of American municipalities have revived it.[28] An Illinois case of 1840 put the argument very clearly: the right of suffrage belongs

> to those who, having by habitation and residence identified their interests and feelings with the citizen, are upon the just principles of reciprocity between the governed and governing, entitled to a vote in the choice of the officers of the government, although they may be neither native nor adopted citizens.[29]

Aliens had to establish a certain degree of residence, but no more than one would have to do in order to appear on the electoral register after moving from Boston to New York.

In the United States, as this quotation illustrates, the practice of permitting aliens to vote could be seen as compatible with the idea of an exclusionary citizenship, but that is a hard balance to maintain. If the vote, of all rights, is in the hands of noncitizens, why should they not count as citizens, and the entire distinction between resident alien and citizen be abandoned? Indeed, something like this thought probably lay behind the disappearance of alien voting: with universal adult citizen suffrage after 1920, the only way to maintain an exclusionary kind of citizenship was to restrict the vote to citizens and not residents. But no theory of "active" democracy can countenance this distinction: the laws concerning our common life must be made by all those who are taking part in it, and residence is the only convincing test of whether someone is taking part—as is understood almost universally when it comes to questions of which citizens should have a voice in local government.

This is something Michael Walzer recognized in *Spheres of Justice* when he observed that "the rule of citizens over non-citizens, of members over strangers, is probably the most common form of tyranny in human history."[30] Walzer has been criticized for arguing from this observation that what he called "communities of character" must be free to decide who joins them from outside, and I think it is fair to say that the position espoused by Joseph Carens, that there should in general be open borders, is now much more popular even among political activists. But it was critical to Walzer's case that there should not be a distinction between citizen and resident, and he understood that this commitment was something that would be difficult to square with open borders. Carens, strikingly, was less concerned with this issue, and talked in *The Ethics of Immigration* in quite conventional terms about the process of naturalization;[31] the idea that an immigrant should be a citizen within a few months of moving does not figure in his account, and one can see why. Both in theory and, even more, in practice, open borders really rely on a strong distinction within the state between citizen and resident, and on the relative powerlessness even of citizens. Would big businesses in the United States (or elsewhere) still welcome large numbers of immigrant workers if they knew that these workers could immediately have political power over them? If all residents are to vote—that is, to become active citizens as soon as possible—it seems to me that *some* kind of immigration policy is necessary, since if this is lacking, it is hard to see how any consistent policies, such as economic planning, can be realized. Politics devolves (as, after all, Sieyès thought ought to be the case) merely into the enforcement of universal human rights, something with which modern market societies long ago made their peace. But the policy should be as liberal as possible, and in particular, it should not (I think) rest on any cultural or ethnic basis. At the moment, the bottleneck for citizenship is (so to speak) internal (precisely the Sieyèsian intention), but it makes better sense from the point of view of radical democracy for it to be at the border. To say this is not, however, to endorse a rich notion of "community" of the Walzerian kind. My own view is that the *only* thing that binds democratic citizens together is that they are engaged in creating through law and politics the conditions of their common life; community in this sense emerges from the activity of collective decision-making rather than needing to precede it. No ethnic or linguistic or cultural criteria are relevant; indeed, I would say that the emphasis on *national* identity as it developed in the nineteenth century was inherently *anti-democratic*, since it required something other than the activity of democracy to be what united citizens, and by doing so it devalued active politics altogether.

VII

A repudiation of representation as the central feature of modern politics has a number of important implications, in addition to its institutional consequences, such as a much greater use of referendums and mandated delegates. Perhaps the most significant implication relates to the continued attempt in twentieth- and twenty-first-century political theory either to find some way of representing the wishes or opinions of individual citizens in some kind of collective form or to show that this is not possible (the most famous of these attempts being Kenneth Arrow's so-called impossibility theorem).[32] Whether it is possible or not, the assumption behind this literature has been that a desirable kind of political arrangement would be one in which wishes or opinions found some kind of representation in the policies adopted by the citizens, and if this turned out to be impossible, it would have quite far-reaching consequences for our politics. On this view, an individual's opinions has to have some causal relationship to the collective outcome, but the relationship might be the same (for example) as the causal relationship between an individual's purchase of something and its future price. Arrow in particular made explicit the fact that the market as well as a voting system might be supposed to generate a social welfare function of the kind he was interested in, and that it too would fail to meet his criteria. A system of opinion polling (to return to the other example I used earlier in this chapter, in contrast to majoritarian voting) might also be a candidate for producing an appropriate function, and it too would fail in the same way.

But if we think of voting not as a way of representing our opinions but as taking part in a collective action that has a specific purpose, where our preferences can be radically altered after the vote has taken place, then the impossibility of these representative systems ceases to matter, since voting (on the Rousseauian picture) should not be a matter of representation *at all*, even in this very broad sense of representation. In an Arrovian welfare function, "individual values are taken as data and are not capable of being altered by the nature of the decision process itself,"[33] as would have to be the case if they are to be represented by the outcome. But Arrow himself contrasted his social choices with those made through strategic behavior on the part of the citizens, or with the alteration of the citizens' preferences to fit in with the need to come to a decision, which would not exhibit the same contradictions, and he even specifically suggested that a Rousseauian approach would avoid his problems.[34]

There is a further and perhaps even more far-reaching implication of what I have been calling an agentive view of democracy. If we were genuinely to be *legislators*, and not people who are *legislated for*, a great deal of how we think about our political life would inevitably change. Imagine forming one's political opinions as if one had in the end to move forward effectively with a majority of one's fellow citizens! We would have to think like democratic citizens, and not like subjects petitioning and protesting, or rulers seeking to exercise power. When Weber (in *The Profession and Vocation of Politics*) described the essence of politics as the ethic of responsibility rather than the ethic of conviction he was, of course, talking to an audience who thought of themselves as one day joining a cadre of professional politicians, set apart from the rest of their nation, and obliged to take responsibility for their actions. But if an entire community were to think of themselves in this way, and to ask the same sort of questions about their beliefs and desires that Weber thought the professional politician had to make, many of the pathologies of modern politics (I say optimistically) might vanish.

As things are, on the other hand, many people form their beliefs in what Weber would have called an irresponsible fashion, without thinking very much about their actual implementation and their consequences—which they leave to their representatives. But (as Marx and the other critics of Sieyèsian politics realized) there cannot be a division of labor of this kind. Although Sieyès and Constant thought that I might have a representative for my politics like I do for my plumbing, so that I tell her what I want and she knows how to do it, political desires are not like that. They are desires for what I want to do with my fellow citizens, and that means I have to think to some extent like the plumber, about what *can* be done, as well as like the householder, who knows what he *wants* to be done. Moreover the "can" here is not a technical question: it is a fundamentally political question, since it turns in great part on what enough of my fellow citizens will accept.

The representatives themselves know this, which is among other things why (unless the political system is on the point of collapse) they understand the need to continue to work with their opponents even after a bitterly fought argument. But a strongly representative system encourages the citizens precisely *not* to think like this, with the result that the gap between the people and their representatives in a democracy grows ever larger. People are encouraged to be "active" citizens, and then at the crucial moment, their activity is blocked and the action is solely in the hands of their representatives; they are *active* but not *decisive*, and that is more *agitation* than *action*.[35] A thorough system of sortition would bring this out even more clearly than a system of elected representatives: a period of lobbying, public debate, et cetera, would be succeeded by a decision made by a small group of people over whom the public would have no control at all, and who they hope would simply "mirror" them. The same is true, and for similar reasons, about methods of constraining legislatures through such things as constitutional courts: these encourage a fundamental irresponsibility on the part of the legislators, since they know that the final decision as to whether a law will be implemented is not in their hands.

Whether these deep features of modern politics can be changed is a question that has lurked unanswered behind much of what I have said in these chapters. As I observed at the end of the first one, there are profound structural reasons why the great democratic movements of the nineteenth and twentieth centuries have not continued into our own time, and why much more intellectual energy has gone into defending restrictions on the naked power of voting than into extending it. If the push for universal suffrage as the means for deciding political and economic questions faltered, it was in part because the social base of a confident democracy had been eroded. Modern conditions of production may never again give people the spectacle of thousands of their fellow citizens engaged in providing them with the necessities of life, and modern warfare will certainly never again call for a mass citizen army. But as I said at the end of my first chapter, our fellow citizens are still there, and they cannot be denied a voice in deciding on the conditions of their lives. What this means in practice depends on quite contingent circumstances: in some cases a greater use of plebiscites, in other cases more effective control of representatives, and so on. But in each of these cases, the key question to be asked is: how in this area can we increase rather than decrease the effectiveness of *voting*, as distinct from other forms of political action or representation. If this were to become our customary approach to political questions, we might even come to see once more that the *only* force capable of countering the enormous power possessed by modern capitalist enterprises over all of us is the force of which they were always most fearful: the actions of an unconstrained and democratic citizenry. At that point we may recover something of the sense of gratitude towards our fellow citizens that we felt a hundred years ago, since it will be they who rescued us from this power.

Comments

3

Democracy as Procedure and Substance

Joshua Cohen

I

Richard Tuck's illuminating chapters on "Active and Passive Citizens" present a defense of "majoritarian democracy."[1] His first chapter introduces our hero, Rousseau, a majoritarian democrat whose conception of democracy has been "regularly misunderstood."[2] Rousseau, correctly understood, was neither utopian dreamer, authoritarian whisperer, nor liberal egalitarian *avant la lettre*. He was instead a radical democrat, committed to democratic politics as a form of collective action that enables people "radically to transform the conditions of their life."[3] His conception of democratic politics comprises voting rights for all who are bound by the laws (including "resident aliens"), a nonrepresentational majoritarianism as the way that citizens rule themselves by making fundamental laws, and an associated hostility to rights entrenched against the majority's legislative judgments.[4]

Our goat, and Rousseau's foil, is Abbé Sieyès, whose thinking has—on Tuck's telling—profoundly shaped the received and truncated wisdom about democratic states. For Sieyès, a state is legitimate when it both protects the fundamental natural and civil rights of all residents of the territory over which it rules and represents the interests of those residents by making laws that advance the general welfare. The institutional means for achieving these twin goals of protecting rights and representing interests are elected legislators with deliberative responsibility—thus freed from mandate—and a constitutional court that protects fundamental rights and perhaps ensures that all interests are indeed represented. Voting rights, which belong only to Sieyèsian active citizens, are a secondary matter, lacking the importance of natural and civil rights and of basic interests. Passive citizens, including women, children, foreigners, and "those who make no contribution to the public establishment," are entitled to what really matters—rights protection and interest representation.[5] In contrast with active citizens, they lack voting rights. But this exclusion reflects a set of political convictions even more fundamental than historical prejudice against the passive. More fundamentally, it reveals the secondary status of political rights in the Sieyèsian conception of the state and political legitimacy.

For Sieyès, then, political legitimacy is fundamentally substantive, about what the state does, not how it does it. For Rousseau, in contrast, political legitimacy is fundamentally procedural: a matter of how decisions are made, not of what is decided. Legitimacy derives from an exercise of sovereignty by active citizens who settle fundamental laws through majority decisions. It depends on us doing something together.

In my remarks, I will sketch a different reading of Rousseau's conception of active citizenship, which I see as a *marriage* of procedure and substance. This alternative reading is, I believe, more faithful to Rousseau's thinking and more plausible than the majoritarian proceduralism that Richard Tuck finds in Rousseau.[6]

II

Rousseau's *Social Contract* is, as his subtitle tells us, about "principles of political right."[7] The "fundamental problem" of political right, he says, is to find "a form of association that will defend and protect the person and goods of each associate with the full common force, *and* by means of which each, uniting with all, nevertheless obey only himself and remain as free as before" (pp. 49–50). I emphasize "and" to draw attention to the two distinct conditions that Rousseau joins in his statement of the fundamental problem: first, that people associate in ways that defend and protect the person and goods of each member (stated more abstractly, their particular interests); and second, that each associate remains "as free as before." "As free as before" here means "morally free," subject only to laws that "one has prescribed to oneself" (p. 54).

In the background of the fundamental problem is the premise that our interests are not fully harmonious but rather partially overlapping and partially conflicting—sufficiently conflicting that "humankind would perish" (p. 49) in the absence of political order. Thus the "opposition of particular interests made the establishment of societies necessary," while "the agreement of these same interests made it possible" (p. 57). What holds a society together—the "social bond," as Rousseau calls it—is "what these different interests have in common." And "it is solely in terms of this common interest that society ought to be governed" (p. 57).

With this background assumption about the nature of our social interdependence, mixing conflicting and common interests, Rousseau offers a solution to the fundamental problem. The solution, laconically stated, is a social compact in which each "puts his person and his full power in common under the supreme direction of the general will" (p. 50). That is "the essence of the social compact." A society under the supreme direction of the general will is a form of association in which citizens share a conception of their common interests or "common good," use that shared understanding as the basis for their political judgments, and treat those political judgments as having priority over judgments about how best to advance their own particular interests. An alternative, more abstract description of the solution is that the associates agree to treat other associates as equals and only to impose burdens on others that they are prepared to live under themselves: they agree to a "condition [that] is equal for all, and since the condition is equal for all, no one has any interest in making it burdensome to the rest" (p. 50). Given the background assumptions about conflicting and common interests, these two formulations amount to the same thing. I will rely here on the formulation that links the general will and the common good.

Rousseau underscores this link between the general will and the common interests of members when he tells us that "what generalizes the [general] will" is "not so much the number of voices, as it is the common interest which unites them" (p. 62). And then, it follows that "it is solely in terms of this common interest that society ought to be governed" (p. 57). So in the society of the general will, the social world guided by principles of political right, members share a commitment to advancing common interests, and that commitment provides "supreme direction" in defining and addressing public matters.

Richard Tuck offers something different. We find no suggestion in Rousseau, he says, "that the building blocks (so to speak) of the general will are anything other than particular wills and private interests; the generality comes, as it did (for example) in Hobbes on democracy, from each citizen's willingness to make the majority will of the society his own, once the vote has taken place."[8] Yes and no. Yes, the common good to which the general will is oriented is constructed out of particular interests: say, for example, each person's particular interest in their own security or well-being. But no, the generality does not come *fundamentally* from a general willingness to accept the decision of the majority as right or legitimate or, still more demandingly, to "make the majority will of the society his own."

Instead, while each of us has an interest in our own security or material well-being, for example, we each (arguably) have an interest in others bearing the costs. The common, generalizable interest to which the general will is oriented is in a system of general security or shared prosperity, the costs of which are covered. That is the generality. To reiterate, "What generalizes the will is not so much the number of voices, as it is the common interest which unites them." Not so much the number of voices, because *a freestanding willingness to accept the decisions of the majority simply does not solve the fundamental problem*, which requires protection for the person and goods of each. "[S]ince each man's force and freedom are his primary instruments of self-preservation, how can he commit them without harming himself, and without neglecting the cares he owes to himself?" (p. 49). Not simply by making the majority will their own. Some assurance is needed that their interests will be defended and protected.

I hear a suspicious voice saying: "So you mean there needs to be a constitutional court that provides such assurance." No, that is not what I mean. What I mean is that there needs to be some assurance. There needs to be because such assurance is part of the intrinsic nature of the general will. That is why "the Sovereign [general will], for its part, cannot burden the subject with any shackles that are useless to the community; it cannot even will to do so" (p. 61). Nothing comparable can be said, under all circumstances, about the decisions of the majority. The problem for Rousseau is to figure out how to ensure that the general will is the supreme authority. No small problem. "The democratic Constitution," he says, "is certainly the Masterpiece of the political art."[9] But it is not resolved by dropping the requirement of assurance.

So we have a problem with two components. And we have a solution, focused on a general will oriented to the common good. But why does that solution solve the problem?

You can see why an association that people agree to must advance their good: without protection for person and goods, we get no ongoing agreement. But why does the solution require a shared understanding of the common good? It is one thing to agree that the association must provide certain universal protections of interests. It is another for members to agree to make that required associational goal their own supreme aim in addressing common affairs.

Why? Well, suppose that the laws of the political society do advance the common interest, and everyone is required to comply with those laws. In the society of the general will, each person endorses that fundamental associational goal. And if you endorse it, then, when you comply with the laws, you follow your own will. That is, by sharing the conception of the common good that the laws are required to advance, members are able to achieve the autonomy that comes from acting on principles they recognize as their own. For citizens to have the general will as a rule is for them to have "their own will alone as rule," and because they have their own will as a rule, "it [the social contract] leaves them as free as before."

So Rousseau's solution is a general willing whose content is an orientation to the common good. That content does not come from the universalizing operations of pure practical reason, but instead from the requirements of achieving both self-legislation and self-protection, under conditions of human interdependence.

III

This more substantive picture of the general will might suggest the spirit of Gudin, who denied, Tuck says, the "radical character of Rousseau's democratic theory" by arguing that "Rousseau's general will represents the general good, and is in principle detachable from the actual process of voting—so that a vote can in effect be nullified if it clashes with what is independently specifiable as the common interest."[10] Or, in a variant denial of radical democratic ambition, it might suggest an epistemic conception of voting, which "preserves the point of voting," but nevertheless "presumes that there is a correct answer to a political question, and that it is the *correctness* of the answer, and not the fact that it was *voted* for, that makes the outcome authoritative."[11]

I am neither embracing these views nor attributing them to Rousseau. To assume otherwise oversimplifies the logical situation. Tuck suggests that we face two mutually exclusive and apparently exhaustive alternatives: a procedure of majority voting is the source of legitimacy or a procedure-independent common good is the source of legitimacy. And if the latter, then voting is either irrelevant or, as in the epistemic view, simply evidentiary.

But it is a mistake to think that these alternatives are exhaustive. Procedure and substance are both important: legislative decisions of the majority and the common good. And when these two come too far apart, "when the general will is no longer the will of all" (p. 122), we cannot simply pick one, because both have roots in the fundamental problem and its solution. Instead, when they come fundamentally apart, we should say that we face a political crisis. Which is pretty much exactly what Rousseau says about majority rule. We find the general will, he says, by counting the votes of the assembled people who express their opinion about what the general will requires. If I am in the minority, I learn that I was wrong. By following the majority, I act on my own will. But those interpretations of the results of majority voting, Rousseau observes, "presuppose, it is true, that all the characteristics of the general will are still in the majority," which means that there is a widely shared concern for the common good. If that is not true, if all the qualities of the general will do not still reside in the majority, then "regardless of which side one takes there is no longer any freedom" (p. 124).

IV

To underscore the distinctiveness of the view I am attributing to Rousseau, I want to say something more about how active citizenship fits into the picture—beyond a mere conformity between a dispersed embrace of the common good and legislation that serves that shared purpose. I think there are four reasons for emphasizing—as Tuck powerfully does—the importance of active citizenship.

First, instrumentally: active citizenship is a means to protect the rights and interests that are ingredient in the common good. It is not conceptually necessary for the protections of your rights and interests that you present them yourself. But on the plausible assumption that you have the best understanding of and most vigilant concern for those interests, we get support for active citizenship. To be clear, having that vigilant concern does not mean that you give undue precedence to your own interests. It simply means that you are vigilant about their due consideration.

Second, Rousseau's most powerful assertions about active citizenship come in his explanation of how the priority of the general will can be preserved in the face of tendencies to subordinate it to particular wills, including the corporate will of government. "As soon as public service ceases to be the Citizens' principal business, and they prefer to serve with their purse rather than with their person, the State is already close to its ruin" (p. 113). The essential idea is that popular assemblies (and I think the idea extends to mandate systems) bring citizens together under manifestly equal conditions, where "the person of the last Citizen is as sacred and inviolable as that of the first Magistrate, because where the Represented is, there no longer is a Representative" (p. 112). This public experience of being treated as an equal reinforces the motivation to express this equality, which lies at the heart of the general will. And to be clear, in the context Rousseau is describing, the person of each (including the "last citizen") is treated as sacred and inviolable not simply by having their rights and interests protected, but because they are deciding along with others on the most fundamental principles of our common association going forward (the laws, in Rousseau's understanding of law as an act of sovereignty, as distinct from policies made by government).

Third, Rousseau does suggest the epistemic virtues of majority decisions addressed to the substance of basic political questions. Under favorable conditions, the majority is more likely to be right about how to advance common interests, and so when you follow them despite having disagreed, you are following your own will.

Finally, perhaps most importantly, Rousseau thinks that citizens must directly and actively exercise responsibility for ensuring the pre-eminence of their sovereign general will in order to have any hope of forestalling the accumulation of independent power in the government. While the government ought to be agent and servant of the sovereign citizens, it tends to operate as an independent agent, usurping sovereign authority. The only obstacle to such usurpation, Rousseau urges, are "the periodic assemblies" of the citizens that he describes in book III of the *Social Contract*. Consider Rousseau's remarkable description, in his 1764 *Letters Written from the Mountain,* of how Geneva's governing small council came to dominate the sovereign people convened in general council: "What happens to all Governments like yours, Gentleman, has happened to you. At first the Legislative power and the executive power that constitute sovereignty are not distinct. The Sovereign People wills by itself, and by itself it does what it wills. Soon the inconvenience of this cooperation of all in everything forces the Sovereign People to charge some of its members to execute its wills. These Officers, after having fulfilled their commission, account for it and return to the common equality. Little by little these commissions become more frequent, finally permanent. Insensibly a body forms that always acts. A body that always acts cannot account for each act: it no longer accounts for any but the principal ones; soon it reaches the point of accounting for none of them. . . . Finally the inaction of the power that wills subjects it to the power that executes. . . . Then there remains in the State only an acting power, that is the executive. The executive power is only force, and where force alone reigns the State is dissolved. There, Sir, is how all democratic States perish in the end."[12]

V

I have been resisting Tuck's account of Rousseau as a majoritarian democrat by emphasizing that Rousseau's view marries procedure and substance. What, then, do I make of the striking passage that

Tuck cites from the end of *Letters Written from the Mountain*: "But above all come together. You are ruined without resource if you remain divided. And why would you be divided when such great common interests unite you? . . . In a word, it is less a question of deliberation here than of concord; the choice of which course you will take is not the greatest question: Were it bad in itself, take it all together; by that alone it will become the best, and you will always do what needs to be done provided that you do so in concert."[13]

My predictable response begins by wondering what it means to do something together, to act in concert, with concord. To put the predictable response more pointedly: Why would we think that this amounts to saying: "But above all follow the vote of the majority?" Or "you will always do what needs to be done provided that you follow the vote of the majority." It strains credulity to think that Rousseau would have found these paraphrases compelling. To be sure, there are circumstances in which the following the decision of the majority will be the way to do things together, to act in concert. But the passage from Rousseau "presupposes that all the characteristics of the general will are still in the majority." When that presupposition fails, *we* do not act *in concert* by following the majority vote. Some of us are subordinate and some are superordinate. And when that is true, "regardless of which side one takes there is no longer any freedom."

VI

Lincoln described democracy as both procedural and substantive, by and for the people. His sense of connection between "by" and "for" was founded on what he described in his First Inaugural as a "patient confidence in the ultimate justice of the people." Perhaps Tuck quietly shares that confidence and hope. If so, then my disagreement is mainly editorial: I simply wish he said something about it. If not, then I am not sure that his account of active citizenship has either the virtues or the Rousseauean pedigree that he claims for it.

4

Passive-Aggressive Citizenship

Melissa Schwartzberg

THE VILLAIN OF RICHARD Tuck's wonderful chapters is the Abbé
Sieyès, theorist of active and passive citizenship. Sieyès justified the
disenfranchisement of all but an estimated one-sixth of the population,[1] defended representation against direct popular participation,
and advocated the entrenchment of constitutional rights, secured by
judicial review. To adapt Tuck's metaphor, Sieyès is the sandman: he
who tucked the sovereign into bed. By contrast, our hero is Jean-
Jacques Rousseau, critic of representation and champion of an in-
somniac sovereign, who insisted upon the participation of the whole
body of citizens in the activity of legislation.[2] Tuck writes that Rousseau not only rejected any possible distinction between active and
passive citizens, but he defended universal suffrage, including female
suffrage.

Let me begin by saying that I share Tuck's broader normative
vision in these chapters, especially in the second. Tuck rightly calls
our attention to the value of majority rule as an expression of equal
political agency. Specifically, he defends a conception of political
agency as realized primarily through the exercise of voting power,
motivated on the individual level by the desire to contribute to an
"efficacious set." This is a deeply compelling response to the ostensible paradox of voting, at once psychologically robust and analyti-
cally precise. Further, I agree with Tuck that especially strenuous
forms of constitutionalism may pose a challenge to democratic

decision-making. But I disagree that Rousseau points the way forward, and I will suggest that in fact Sieyès is a more plausible source for Tuck's "efficacious set" logic of democratic decision-making. The lens of female suffrage clarifies all of this, and so I will use it as a basis for exploring the underlying question of political agency. For Sieyès, the status of the "stakeholder" against aristocratic power provided a claim for expanded suffrage rights and extended the honorific status of citizen to those who would otherwise be deemed mere subjects. For Rousseau, because citizenship required a demanding set of moral and political capacities, not all those within a republic could become citizens; some would necessarily remain subjects. In the contemporary world, many members of political communities still are subjects, rather than citizens; even "active" citizens mainly monitor the performance of their representatives and seek to undermine attempts at domination through indirect means. But this means that the "passive" versus "active" citizen dichotomy actually occludes a primary behavioral strategy of members of modern states: passive-aggression.

———

To begin, it is certainly true that in the famous July 1789 address on *The Rights of Man and the Citizen*, Sieyès held that women ought not to have an "active influence" on the state (*chose publique*). However, even in the passage Tuck cites, there is a caveat: "at least as things stand at the moment" (*du moins dans l'état actuel*). The provisional character of women's exclusion is not extended to the others so identified—children and foreigners. These groups are excluded, according to Sieyès, because only those who "contribute to the public establishment" can be active citizens. But by the time of his October 1789 "Observations on the Report of the Constitutional Committee," Sieyès argued that the exclusion of women in fact could not be justified except by reference to unfounded prejudice:

> According to present mores, opinions, and human institutions, women are allowed to wear the crown; but by a bizarre contradiction, they are not permitted any share of active citizenship, as if a healthy polity should not always try to increase the proportion of

active citizens, or, as if it is impossible that a woman could ever be of utility to the public interest. It is due to a prejudice that cannot even be challenged that we are forced to exclude at least half of the population.[3]

There were few champions of female suffrage in this period. But Sieyès, at least, recognized that the exclusion of women from active citizenship was unjustified, resting merely on prejudice rather than on any well-grounded belief in women's inability to participate.

To be sure, Sieyès was no Marquis de Condorcet. Condorcet consistently argued that women's apparent incompetence derived not from their nature but their lack of education—that they were equally capable as men of reason and of moral ideas—and passionately defended women's right to active citizenship. In his "Second Letter from a Freeman of New Haven to a Citizen of Virginia on the Futility of Dividing the Legislative Power among Several Bodies," Condorcet compared the exclusion of women to the status of subject populations in republics and bemoaned the neglect of their rights, writing:

> Even a philosopher finds it hard not to get a little carried away when discussing women. However, I fear that I shall fall foul of them if ever they read this article. I have discussed their right to equality and not their influence, and so might be suspected of secretly wishing to decrease this influence. And since Rousseau gained their support by saying that they were made simply to look after us and were fit only to torment us, I should not expect their support. But truth is a good thing, even if I lay myself open to ridicule by speaking it.[4]

In a remarkable act of interpretive charity—of which I cannot find myself capable—Tuck argues that we should not presume that Rousseau intended to exclude women from the category of citizenship, in part because Rousseau must have known that at least some women did in fact vote in France, Corsica, and perhaps even Geneva. Let's assume that Tuck is correct, and that Rousseau was indeed aware of this. But this is why it is all the more striking that nowhere did he ever explicitly defend women's participation and was identified as being a deliberate hindrance to the cause by Condorcet.

Why would Sieyès have been, at least in principle, more willing than Rousseau to extend political rights to (some) women? The answer rests on their respective justifications for the right to vote, and on how they each construed the scope of political agency. To begin, the distinction between active and passive citizenship, for Sieyès, did not rest on competence but on the status of being a "stakeholder" in the community. Active citizens were akin to those who had shares as "members of the association"—those who paid an annual sum in direct taxation equal to three days' local wages—whereas passive citizens benefited from the society without having such a stake. Some, like Dupont Nemours, resisted Sieyès's too expansive account of active citizenship, arguing that the true stakeholders were property owners.[5] But for Sieyès, the crucial criterion was freedom from economic dependence, rather than competence. Indeed, this criterion endured: even in 1792—when the distinction between active and passive citizens was abolished and quasi-universal male suffrage ushered in— eligibility for the franchise was restricted to men twenty-one years of age and older "living upon an income or from the proceeds of employment, and not working as a domestic servant."[6]

To be sure, the wider logic of representation, both in Sieyès's writings and in the 1791 Revolutionary Constitution, depended on distinction and eminence, notably in the system of indirect elections and the higher tax qualification for electors.[7] But the Constitution of 1791 imposed no other "competence" checks on active citizens apart from having reached the age of maturity.[8] For Sieyès, the requirement of special competence was for elected representatives—those who had responsibility for promoting the interests of the citizenry— rather than for voters, and so the grounds on which active and passive citizens were distinguished rested on tax payment as a marker of stakeholding rather than capacity, as such. Insofar as women were financially dependent on men or deprived of property or inheritance rights, they could not meet the criteria. But Sieyès did not argue that women could not as a matter of nature, or capacity, serve as active citizens.

In contrast, Rousseau offered just this argument, as the above passage from Condorcet observed. Citizenship depended upon a particular form of republican virtue, inaccessible to many members of a political community (and some communities in toto). Rousseau intended not merely to strip participatory rights from members who would not make the civil profession of faith but to banish them, because one could not be "either a good Citizen or a loyal subject" without it.[9] Moreover, as the discussion of the Lawgiver suggests, not every community is ripe for citizenship: "For Nations as for men there is a time of maturity for which one has to wait before subjecting them to laws."[10] For example, Peter the Great did not see that the Russians lacked the "maturity for political order," and sought to make them Germans and Englishmen before Russians, thereby "preventing his subjects from ever becoming what they could be by persuading them that they are what they are not."[11]

For Rousseau, not every adult member of a community possessed the capacity to participate as a full political agent. And—so far as women were concerned—their appropriate role in political society was as helpmeet and as moral educators of children, not as citizens. But this did not shield them from responsibility for the fostering of republican virtue. Indeed, in *Emile*, he argues at length that the possibility of moral reform and the fate of all social institutions rests upon their willingness to breastfeed their children.[12]

Given that the republic rested on women, and on mothers in particular, perhaps Rousseau did not believe that women *by nature* were incompetent and incapable of serving as citizens. But he denied that women ought to be trained to develop the ability to serve as citizens: men should be "active and strong," and women should be "passive and weak."[13] Rather, they needed to acquire the proper training to serve as subjects. In part, this must entail "a profound study of the mind of men—not an abstraction of the mind of man in general, but the minds of men around her, the minds of men to whom she is subjected by either law or opinion (*l'esprit des hommes auxquels elle est assujettie, soit par la loi, soit par l'opinion*)."[14]

Even if this is not misogyny, it is clearly far from citizenship. Women are specifically described as mere *subjects*, described in *Social Contract* as those who are subjected to the laws of the State, as opposed to Citizens, "participants in the sovereign authority."[15] From a political standpoint, they could not have equal standing. In *Emile*, he insisted that when women complain about "unjust man-made inequality, she is wrong. This inequality is not a human institution—or, at least, it is the work not of prejudice but of reason."[16] Moreover, "Wherever she makes use of her rights, she has the advantage. Wherever she wants to usurp ours, she remains beneath us."[17]

Although the association of virtue with republicanism is not unique to Rousseau, it is hard not to see in the Jacobins' conception of virtue at least some of the distinctive features of Rousseauian thought. Specifically, in 1793, the Committee of General Security considered whether women should exercise political rights or be able to participate in political clubs; the committee opposed such rights on the grounds that women lacked the "moral and physical qualities" to do so.[18] Such Rousseauian sentiments were publicized in an "Avis aux Républicaines" in the *Feuille du Salut Public*:

> Women! Do you want to be Republicans? . . . Be simple in your dress, hardworking in your homes, never go to the popular assemblies wanting to speak there. But let your occasional presence there encourage your children. Then *la Patrie* will bless you, for you will have done for it what it has a right to expect from you.[19]

This is not Sieyès—this is Rousseau, through and through.

I have argued that Rousseau clearly believed that women did not possess the qualities necessary for citizenship. But now I want to suggest that this was in part due to the morally demanding quality of participation in the republic of equals, though here too I will depart from Tuck's account. Tuck argues that in the key passages of *Social Contract*, Rousseau sought not to reject the aggregation of private, individual interests—the "will of all"—but merely the introduction of partial societies. On his reading, citizens are not required to think about the common good as they vote; rather, they are merely obliged to obey the vote of the majority, by which the general will is ascertained. In Tuck's words, this is "perfectly compatible with it being the case that people vote in their own interests." This is a plausible and appealing account of political obligation. But it does not seem consistent with the claims in *Social Contract*.

Rousseau repeatedly wrote that citizens must set aside their private or particular interests to focus on what is advantageous to the community. In his words at book I chapter 7, "Indeed, each individual may, as a man, have a particular will contrary to or different from the general will he has as a Citizen. His particular interest may speak to him quite differently from the common interest."[20] But when he votes—as Tuck of course recognizes—a citizen should say, "it is advantageous to the State," not "it is advantageous to this man or to this party that this or that opinion pass. Thus the law of public order in assemblies consists not so much in upholding the general will in them, as in seeing to it that the general will is always consulted and that it always replies."[21] Now, it is surely true that in a well-ordered society, the general will should not differ much from the will of all. This is why Rousseau paid so much attention to the mores and habituation of citizens to virtue: the goal was to adapt their view of their private interest in such a way that it would not typically diverge from the common interest. But where they did diverge, Rousseau was unambiguous; citizens must orient themselves toward the common interest as they vote, not fall back on their private interest.

The general will does not merely generate an obligation on the part of the minority to accept the result of the majority decision, as Tuck also suggests. Rather, those in the minority must recognize—in epistemic and moral humility—that they *erred* in their judgment of the general will.[22] This is clear from book IV chapter 2: "Therefore when the opinion contrary to my own prevails, it proves nothing more than that I made a mistake and that what I took to be the general will was not. If my particular opinion had prevailed, I would have done something other than what I had willed, and it is then that I would not have been free."[23]

To be sure, this does not necessarily imply an "epistemic reading" of the sort that Tuck rightly rejects; it doesn't mean that there is a "right answer" to a political problem, in the contemporary sense of that term. But it does suppose that there *is* a right answer as to whether a proposed law is consistent with the general will of the specific community; put differently, this "right answer" may vary across communities, all of which have different general wills. The ability of a majority to reliably discern the general will in a particular community did depend upon a healthy body politic; that is, one in which "all the characteristics of the general will are still in the majority: once they no longer are, then regardless of which side one takes there no longer is any freedom."[24] Only in well-ordered communities will the vote of the majority reliably reveal the general will.

The reason why Rousseauian citizenship is demanding is not just because it involves ongoing participation in acts of sovereignty. Rather, it is *morally* demanding—it requires us to orient ourselves through virtue (hence the Legislator and the civic faith) towards the well-being of the community as a whole. This is a standard that women, on Rousseau's account, cannot meet. Were it merely the case that women needed only to consult their own interest, they could be capable of citizenship. But because the duties of citizens are so oner-ous from the standpoint of virtue, women can only be deemed incompetent.

In the second chapter, Tuck draws on his account of Rousseau to defend the logic of the "efficacious set," by which each citizen can feel that she has causally contributed to the attainment of a sufficient number of votes to achieve some desired result. Again, I believe this to be an attractive and important account of individual agency in democratic decision-making. But it is not Rousseau's. As I have ar-gued, this is the logic of the will of all, not the general will: what generalizes the will is not a specific proportion of the sum of indi-vidual votes, even if a community relies upon a given majority or qualified-majority threshold to reveal it.[25] For Rousseau, the general will "is not so much the number of voices, as it is the common interest which unites them."[26]

In fact, Tuck's argument is much closer to Sieyès's own account of the relationship between the common will and majority rule. Sieyès's "Views of the Executive Means" provides the less demanding version of the general will that Tuck ascribes to Rousseau. There, Sieyès held that the common will "cannot consist of anything other than the citi-zens' individual wills," subject to the obligation to abide by the major-ity of those wills.[27] He argued that every citizen must see himself as "bound by the majority view even when his own will forms part of the minority."[28] In contrast to Rousseau, a citizen who finds him-self to be in the minority need not believe himself to be mistaken; he need only take himself to be obliged to go along with the majority decision.

Sieyès also provided a defense of equal political agency that is strikingly similar to Tuck's own majoritarianism. He held that the representative assembly must be arranged on equal terms, arguing against the proposal by moderate deputies that legislative power should be checked by allocating veto power to each of the two houses of a bicameral legislature, and by assigning the king veto power over both. Rejecting the moderates' preoccupation with ongoing sovereignty, Sieyès instead argued on behalf of a constituted order grounded on equality among citizens: a legislative veto to the monarch would treat his vote as weightier than any other citizen, and bicameralism itself reflected a division of society into orders, rather than as a body of individual and equal citizens.[29] In *What Is the Third Estate?*, he insisted that the Third Estate was not merely one of the "three orders" but a complete nation; further, the deputies of the clergy and nobility were not the representatives of the Nation and so should not have a right to vote on its behalf. Were they to vote by order, the will of the privileged individuals could overwhelm those of the twenty-five million citizens comprising the Third Estate. But then he continued:

> If votes were taken by *head*, with each privileged and non-privileged vote having an equal weight, this would still mean that the will of two hundred thousand individuals would match those of twenty-five million, because they would have an equal number of representatives. But is it not monstrous to compose an assembly in such a way as to enable it to vote in favor of the interest of a minority? Surely this must be the *reverse* of an assembly?[30]

This seems to me to be quite close to Tuck's considered position in the second chapter, with which I wholeheartedly agree: if a minority regularly prevailed over a majority, as under supermajority or unanimity rule, then any particular member of the community would be likely to have less agency than were the decision to be taken in accordance with the wishes of the majority.

It is surely true that a representative system leaves the vast majority of citizens in the position of relative passivity, as mere electors (or, in Sieyès's indirect system, as electors of electors). But it is also true that the demands of political judgment in a well-ordered republic, for Rousseau, required the exclusion of whole categories of persons. And whereas Sieyès's theory prescribed a role for those persons as "passive citizens," and advocated for an equal system of representation, Rousseau took those who were ineligible to participate to be mere subjects. Rousseau's account may have the merit of transparency—those who do not participate in the creation of the law are unfree, and calling them "passive citizens" obfuscates the matter. But this ought not to count in favor of a view of Rousseau as a theorist of universal suffrage.

———

We are left to ask if we should describe the modern citizen as active or passive, given the limited role for direct political participation in contemporary representative democracies. If constitutional rigidity and inegalitarian representative schemes constitute forms of domination, as Tuck reasonably suggests, how should we characterize citizens' agency? Throughout his work, James Scott has carefully documented the strategies of those who deploy veiled means of subversion against powerful actors, analyzing the "hidden transcripts" of those who engage in "down-to-earth, low-profile stratagems" like foot-dragging, theft, and shirking.[31] One way to characterize these strategies is to use the psychological category of "passive aggression": resistant behavior that cannot be expressed openly.[32]

Consider the *tricoteuses* at the guillotine, memorialized by Charles Dickens in *Tale of Two Cities* in the character of Madame Defarge, knitting the names of those to be executed into her scarf. Neither active nor strictly passive, the *tricoteuses* knitted both while they sat in the galleries at the assembly debates and while they cheered for the blood of their enemies. How should we characterize their agency? On the one hand, their noisy presence regularly disrupted the proceedings at the assembly, mocking moderate deputies and other attendees. On the other hand, they were excluded from meaningful political participation, and so they acted within their constraints, working through acts of sabotage and menace.[33]

Beyond the *tricoteuses*, knitting has a long and distinguished history as a mechanism of female resistance. The creation of pink pussyhats in response to Donald Trump's election—after the release of a videotape in which he gleefully admitted to grabbing women's genitals—is merely the most recent example. In response to the 1765 Stamp Act, female colonists formed an auxiliary to the Sons of Liberty resisters to promote the boycott of British wares by creating "homespun" goods. Spinning and knitting bees abounded. Milcah Martha Moore spoke for the women resisters in lines from her "Patriotic Poesy":[34]

> Let the Daughters of Liberty, nobly arise
> And tho' we've no Voice, but a negative here
> The use of the Taxables, let us forbear . . .
> Join mutual in this, and but small as it seems
> We may jostle a Grenville and puzzle his Schemes . . .

Tuck suggests that, at least between elections, we are not truly active citizens—it is our legislators who do the meaningful work of acting together. But neither are we (adult) citizens truly passive, deprived of the rights of political agency: instead, our disenfranchised members, including those who are undocumented and those with felony convictions, fall into that category. When we are not engaged in the act of voting, we are largely preoccupied with surveilling, tweeting, and knitting. Perhaps, like the women of revolutionary France, we are passive-aggressive citizens.

5

Tuck's Democracy

John Ferejohn

RICHARD TUCK ARGUES in chapters 1 and 2 that modern democracies are really no such thing. Most, he says, have followed Abbé Sieyès in adopting a form of government, based on elected representatives, in which the "effective" citizenship is reserved to a small fraction of the people who have the political rights or capacities to play an active role in government. The rest remain passive citizens who enjoy some security and welfare and protection of civil rights, but whose role in government is confined to periodic (and not very frequent) elections. He traces Sieyès's legacy through Hegel, Guizot, and Mill and, in our own day, to Joseph Schumpeter and others who defend what many have called minimal or "elitist" versions of democracy. Bernard Manin has described this system in detail in his book on representative government, and many defend it as the best feasible kind of democracy for a modern state. Moreover, at least since World War II, modern states have increasingly adopted rigid, judicially enforceable constitutions with the effect of guaranteeing the protection of the rights of both passive and active citizens, and specifically against the actions of the majority.

Tuck regards modern Sieyèsian government, constitutional representative government, as profoundly undemocratic and argues in favor what he calls radical (majoritarian) democracy—advancing a theory of what he calls a "Rousseauian" kind against its modern critics. Tuck builds his theory on a novel conception of "active citizenship"

in which, he claims, individuals can see themselves as causally responsible in some way for the laws—or at least the newly enacted
laws. Insofar as most people can think of themselves plausibly
as active citizens in this way, Tuck says that the laws will be legitimate because the people would be living under laws they "made."
Active citizenship, he argues, is both an attractive and feasible idea
for the modern democratic state. If citizens embraced this self-
conception, individuals would be amply motivated to exercise their
political rights as active citizens and in that respect, live under laws
of their own making.

Tuck also insists that everyone who lives (legally?) in the country and is subject to its laws, must be allowed a genuine role in
making them. Each (adult) resident—male, female, alien, or
native—must therefore be enfranchised in order to make law with
others on equal terms. Tuck recognizes that by permitting the vote
to all legal residents, there would have to be regulation of movement at the borders and an immigration policy that assures that
those who come are committed to living together with others on
equal terms. This policy, he hopes, will be as liberal as possible, but
if I understand his conception correctly, I am not sure how liberal
it can be.

Tuck allows that we may, for practical reasons, choose to elect representatives to parliament so that they may (perhaps?) debate and
develop legislative proposals and may (in the end) formally enact the
laws. But these representatives, he argues, ought to be instructed delegates, whose duty is to execute the instructions conveyed to them
by their constituents. He seems to agree with Rousseau that laws
should be general, more like constitutional provisions rather than
ordinary legislation. Besides, construing laws as pertaining to constitutional essentials—which might be few in number and general in
scope—makes plausible the notion that ordinary people would have
views on those matters and that representatives could be instructed
to act on those views. If there is a chance that representatives may
stray from their remit, perhaps instructions would need to backed up
with recall elections (as in California) but Tuck seems not to require
this. These institutional ideas are not really developed much here

beyond hints from and an implicit reliance on Rousseau's political works to help fill in the blanks. Tuck's institutional principles seem to be these:

1. (generality) Each person should be treated equally by the law (as a subject); laws are general/abstract "constitutional" provisions.
2. (democracy in one country) Each (adult legal) resident should have an equal role in lawmaking activity, subject to legal residence being regulated at the borders.
3. (radical democracy) Laws (principle 1) are made either by direct majority vote among those eligible to vote (principle 2) or by elected representatives acting according to instructions given them by their constituents (principle 2).

    These principles are consistent with and supported by what seems to be a moral principle:

4. (active democracy) Each person regards him- or herself as obliged to exercise his or her right to vote actively by playing the part of an agent in making the laws together with others.[1]

I have several questions. In section I, I ask whether Rousseau's institutional prescriptions provide much help for Tuck's radical democracy project. First, despite what French revolutionaries may have thought, it is very hard to see Rousseau as committed to either to *equality* in voting or to democratic *government*. While the sovereign must approve any law by voting, it is not clear that the voting rule would weigh each vote equally.[2] Second, It is not clear to me that the Rousseaian institutional principles 1 and 3 actually constrain the government from acting arbitrarily. If laws must be general and abstract, as Rousseau and Tuck demand, government officials must retain authority to interpret laws in order to apply or follow them. Moreover, the sovereign, as such, seems to lack any "legal" way of responding to particular governmental acts by, for example, striking down offending decrees. Such an action would necessarily be particular rather than general. Moreover, while elected representatives are to be restricted to following instructions in making general laws, are they also restricted in any way when undertaking magisterial activity (enacting day-to-day particular legislation and appropriations and decrees, which form most of the activity of a modern parliament)?

In section II, I explore Tuck's agentic view of politics and argue that what makes Tuck's radical democracy attractive is its foundation in the moral principle of active agency. Unless people see themselves as having the obligation to take an active responsibility for the laws in the way that principle 4 requires, radical democracy seems more dangerous than alluring.

Section III concerns diversity and the treatment of minorities both outside the country (seeking residence) and inside (seeking protection against repression). How is principle 2 supposed to work? Presumably the state must have the authority to restrict entry to assure that those who enter are suitably committed to common purposes. This may be a very demanding and potentially quite illiberal requirement. Potential entrants might need to show they are morally worthy of citizenship. Rousseau's recommendations as to how Poland should treat its serfs may provide some guidance. He recommends treating them as supplicants asking for admission and not as rights-bearers. Moreover, is state policy to be restricted only to admitting (some of) those people who appear to be committed to active citizenship of the kind Tuck recommends? Or may the failure to conform to the morality of active citizenship also justify expulsions of those already in the community? Then, whatever law the people, as sovereign, enact concerning immigration, how does that actually constrain governmental interpretation and enforcement either at the border or when considering the treatment of historically oppressed minorities (the Polish serfs again)?

I

Rousseau's political writings were addressed to very different political contexts. I think this is important in interpreting his often cryptic recommendations and observations. In *The Social Contract*, Rousseau sets out general maxims for constructing a polity that would produce legitimate law—so that people would be living under laws of their own making. His recommendation, roughly, was that legislation should be "democratic" but government should be (for most communities) conducted by an elective aristocracy. In *Poland* he confronts a large heterogeneous and very unequal polity with a large class of serfs and recommends enfranchising only the major and minor nobility, leaving the issue of the serfs for another day.[3] Essentially, his recommendations for Poland more or less resembled classical institutions of the Roman republic (with a senate, comitia, elected officials, and censors to regulate citizenship) and instructed delegates in an elected legislature. In the *Letters*, he addresses citizens who confront a government that has already unjustly usurped legislative powers, and he tries to improvise ways (based on his reading of old Genevan documents) to give the people some hope (however slim) of recovering their rightful powers.

Tuck says that "Rousseau's fundamental idea was that no law carries obligation for us unless we have actually taken part in making it." This may be given either a collectivist or individualist interpretation. A collectivist interpretation would be that law binds "us" only if "we" (together) have taken part in making it.[4] Quoting from *The Social Contract*: "every law that the people has not ratified in person is null and void—is, in fact, not a law." Tuck's own interpretation, however, puts the matter both individualistically and voluntaristically: "The central convictions of writers and activists in this tradition have been, first, that if *I* have not *played a part* in legislating, laws have no authority over *me*" (chap. 2 sec. I).[5] A collective interpretation of Rousseau's passage seems most plausible to me: Rousseau says only that the "people" (acting together in some official way) must ratify a proposed law in person.[6]

Tuck's interpretation seems more like (philosophical) anarchism than democracy: if I were to decline (or forget) to take part in law making, then law produced by my community has no authority for me and I must make my own moral judgments about how to act. Contrast this with Rousseau's argument (which Tuck accepts) that even if I voted against a law that the community agreed to, I should see my own vote as incorrect and take the community's judgment as my own. But suppose I had declined to vote; or, if it rained and I was prevented from voting? Wouldn't it still be the case that I should take the community's judgment as my own and (whether I did that or not) regard the law as obligating me? That I would be so obligated follows naturally from the "epistemic" interpretation of Rousseau that Tuck rejects. On that view, the general will is part of your will, and a law voted by the people is very likely to conform to the general will, whether you voted for or against it or voted at all. Failure (or refusal) to vote or participate does not seem to excuse you from accepting that inference.[7]

Tuck points out in chapter 1 that Rousseau used the term *law* very differently from the way legislative acts are understood today. Tuck says, "The laws that we have to ratify in person are fundamental ones, closer to constitutional articles, rather than the day-to-day business of a Parliament or Congress" (sec. III). For Rousseau, laws "have to be general in *scope* as well as general in origin" (ibid.). I understand *scope generality* to be a substantive rather than merely formal requirement. Valid laws could not apply to particular people, places, occupations, and so on, however implicitly. They must in fact apply to everyone equally. Today, most legislatures mostly eschew substantive requirements of this kind—except to the extent that tests of constitutionality exist—and say that any procedurally valid enactment by Parliament or Congress (in the elaborate way specified in the US Constitution) is considered to be a law.

To be a law therefore, a proposition must be something like a general prohibition of murder or rape, for example, or perhaps a proposal to establish an institution of some kind (such marriage, or a regime of enforceable contracts), or a program to build a highway system, or to establish an office or an agency. Laws however could not award contracts, site the highways, or appoint or elect officials. Rousseau in his discussion of the "lawgiver" also dwells on the special case of a law establishing a community or a form of government, which (like any law) must be ratified by the people if it is to be "their" government. If a proposition fails the generality test—and deals with particulars—it cannot be a law at all even if a majority votes for it, because it cannot be an expression of the *general* will.[8]

Even if the sovereign monopolizes the lawmaking power, and decides on laws by casting votes, it is not clear that votes must be equally weighted—that decisions are to be taken by simple majority voting. Indeed, the thrust of his republican examples (Sparta, Rome, etc.)

and his recommendations in *Poland* should make one skeptical that he thought votes must be equal (or available to every resident). In this sense, Rousseau's commitment to "democratic" lawmaking seems quite weak.

Rousseau famously insisted on distinguishing government from the sovereign (the people).[9] While the laws must be made by the sovereign, it is up to the government to implement the laws and govern the country for the common good. Legislation is meant to empower and direct government, but most acts of government—then and now—require that the government interpret the laws and exercise discretion in applying them. Insofar as laws are confined to stating general principles—something like the equal protection clause or the First Amendment—there remains immense room for governmental interpretation. This is especially true when the sovereign is not actually present, as will often be the case, or if it is in some way inhibited from interfering with the application and interpretation of laws. Rousseau does not propose (until the *Letters*) any way that governmental discretion can be limited other than by the self-restraint of the magistrates themselves. In fact, any such interference would be a particular act and not available to the sovereign. Rousseau asserts that the people—as sovereign—cannot convene itself.[10] Unless the usurpation is noticed by a regular meeting of the sovereign—a matter of pure chance, at best—there seem to be no regular means by which sovereign action can be taken against a rogue government.[11] In the Eighth and Ninth Letters from the Mountain, Rousseau insisted that the people of Geneva had a right of *remonstrance* when the government usurps legislative authority.[12] This right, however, they have only as individuals or groups and not as sovereign. Remonstrance, moreover, is emphatically not a power to make laws; laws can only be made by the people together in a legally convened assembly and only on subjects satisfying scope generality. Remonstrance is, at most, only a power to prevent the government from illegal innovations insofar as the government can be required to address them in some institutional way. But until there is a law requiring that, it is hard to see what the citizens of Geneva could do.

Moreover, while the sovereign—the assembled people—must act directly to make law by some form of majority rule, it is not clear to me that this implies any commitment to equality in voting. It is a mistake to think that majority rule implies either a wide suffrage or simple or equal weighted majority voting. Certainly, Rousseau's favored examples—the classical republics of Sparta and Rome—excluded vast numbers of people from the franchise and, in the case of Rome, invariably employed wealth-weighted voting. It is true they used some form of majority rule, but votes were not equal. In this respect, Roman voting was rather like voting shares in corporate elections.

If the people choose to institute an elective aristocracy—which is the form of government Rousseau thinks appropriate in most places and which the Genevans had done—the magistrates are told by the sovereign to *do anything you decide is necessary to govern well under the general laws.*[13] In other words, *the sovereign leaves matters to the self-restraint of the magistrates.* Rousseau thought, however, that elections would produce "uprightness, understanding, experience and all other claims to pre-eminence . . . it is the best and most natural arrangement that the wisest should govern the many, when it is assured that they will govern for its profit, and not for their own." But he cautions that "if aristocracy does not demand all the virtues needed by popular government, it demands others which are peculiar to itself; for instance, moderation on the side of the rich and content-ment on that of the poor; for it seems that thorough-going equality would be out of place, as it was not found even at Sparta" (III.5). Plainly, this did not work in Geneva, as the magistrates gradually took away the powers of the sovereign. The sovereign could not convene itself and, even if it happened to be meeting, it cannot repeal or over-ride particular decrees by acts of law. Rousseau had little more to say. The "People" could not act together but must resist encroachment as individuals remonstrating. This would require individual insight and courage—virtues he thought was in short supply in Geneva.

II

In his second chapter, where he advances his own *agentic* view of politics, Professor Tuck seems to depart somewhat from Rousseau's generality requirement for collective action and puts his emphasis on the *decision* to take collective action. He says, in effect, that *whatever* the majority decides is law and is, therefore, part of the general will *by that fact alone.* At the start of the chapter: "democracy is best understood as a means of collective *action*, giving human beings the capacity radically to transform the conditions of their life. On this view, the essential characteristic of democratic politics is that the citizens are aware of themselves as engaged in constructing this common activity, and are willing to allow the wishes of a majority to override their own wishes" (sec. I).

Tuck relies on Rousseau's remark at the end of *Letters Written from the Mountain:* "it is less a question of deliberation here than of concord; the choice of which course you will take is not the greatest question: Were it bad in itself, take it all together; by that alone it will become the best" (sec. I). Tuck says, "One way of capturing what is implied in the agentive view is precisely that it takes democracy to be in effect a kind of civilized and domesticated version of a mob—and that should not alarm us. . . . The great discovery of democracy was that people could accept a simple head count as the basis for the transformation which they might otherwise have effected through physical action and, potentially, violence" (chap. 2 sec. V).

These are, it seems to me, genuine expressions of radical democracy in the sense that there seems no limit to the people's lawmaking powers. They echo Xenophon's quotation when someone protested illegally trying the generals collectively: "the majority kept crying out that it was monstrous if the people were to be hindered by any stray individual from doing what seemed to them right" (*Hellenica* book I). These expressions in Geneva and Athens seem to be by a people facing injustice and denied their proper role as sovereign, as the Genevans were in 1762–63. In that context, Rousseau was not urging that the people of Geneva make new laws. They could not because they were not able to assemble. He was urging them to do *something*, to take action to interfere with the injustice. Rousseau was appealing to the citizens of Geneva—or actually to the middle class—to take matters into their own hands and remonstrate against the illegal conduct of the small council (the government), perhaps provoking it to convene the General Council (seemed a long shot). In that kind of situation, Tuck is right, the alternative to doing something about injustice is doing nothing; there is no time to quibble over details. But what lessons do these circumstances—circumstances of injustice—have for how we should arrange our public affairs when setting up a new republic?

In the context of the *Social Contract*, Rousseau sought to establish well-functioning and more or less just social arrangements on a clean slate. Should such a society decide to institute a civil state, the people should retain the authority make their own laws, and the (elective aristocratic) government should act to further the public welfare in ways consistent with those laws. Because the government would normally be composed of well-intentioned and able magistrates, it would normally resist the urge to usurp the legislative authority. But even in the context of *The Social Contract*, Rousseau recognized that the temptations of government are to aggrandize its powers, and as government is always in session while the sovereign rarely is, this temptation may not always be resisted. In this circumstance, the people must be willing to take matters upon themselves, as individuals or small groups, when the sovereign cannot act. Improvised mob action, which might well be needed in some cases to save the constitution, would not constitute legislation, in Rousseau's sense.

Tuck may believe that Rousseau's system is too austere for our times. Our parliaments have to be able to act on particulars as well as on general propositions. The complexity and scale of the modern state may demand no less. He notes approvingly that "the history of the United Kingdom, at least down to the 1970s, is an often overlooked vindication of rather pure majoritarianism" (chap. 2 sec. IV). But the United Kingdom has a modern parliament with a wide remit, able to do anything it chooses except to turn a man into a woman (nowadays that is not a limit). But how well does that parliament fit Tuck's democratic aspirations? A majority of the parliament is not the same as a majority of the people. Leaving aside the mathematics of the electoral system, when is the last time the prime minister's party received a majority of the electorate? And how much actual control does the parliament have over the conduct of its government? Its members will tell you that they are, for the most part, a kind of electoral college to choose the prime minister and cabinet and who, as MPs, are mostly steered through the voting lines at governmental command. Their role is largely limited to expressing confidence, which allows the cabinet the main role in devising laws and enforcing them. No doubt, it is a bit more democratic than the US government but—with its malapportioned Senate and Electoral College, and a Supreme Court empowered to strike down statutes—the United States cannot even pretend to be a simple democracy.

Still, I think Tuck's notion of active democracy (as I understand it) remains attractive and not just for mobbing. The attraction, however, seems limited to a world in which the citizens (and residents) are morally motivated in certain way and where they share thick common interests sufficient to hold them into a community of (more or less) equals. Tuck's example is drawn from the logic of collective action in the context of voting where, on standard economic analysis, if the voting act is costly, no one (or almost no one in a game-theoretic model) has an incentive to vote because the chance of a person's vote being decisive (or pivotal) in changing the outcome is effectively zero. Tuck argues, however, that each person's vote can (in a sense) be sufficient to bring about her desired outcome. Suppose a person preferred A to B and voting took place sequentially. Then in any sequence in which A received $m - 1$ votes (where m is sufficient for a majority) the person's vote would be decisive because it would be *sufficient* to put A over the top. This argument also applies to simultaneous (or anonymous) as well as sequential voting in any set of ballots in which my preferred candidate received $m - 1$ votes since my vote would be (pivotal) sufficient, whether or not I know it. I would rationally recognize that my vote makes a difference only in those ballot configurations, in which case I should always vote for my preferred option (it is a weakly dominant strategy). Tuck then argues, if I want to be an "agent" in the sense of contributing to the success of my preferred alternative, sufficiency gives me an instrumental reason to vote "if my vote is *sufficient* . . . I have to have the further or 'meta' desire that it should be I who is bringing about the result" (chap. 2 sec. III). In effect, my desire to be agentic in Tuck's sense—which is a kind of moral motivation—makes the voting act costless to me (or actually beneficial) and, given that I will vote for this reason, I have sufficient reason to vote my preferred alternative. Tuck acknowledges that "There is, of course, an element of what might be thought of as expressiveness in this, in that I am motivated by the value to me of the action; but it is only of value to me *because* it is instrumental, and because I can rightly think I am achieving something directly through my vote" (ibid.).

I agree with all this. If agents are morally motivated in this way—to be active contributors to the collective life—they may have reason to vote and, in other ways, act as good citizens. Perhaps as citizens of Geneva they should also be prepared to risk their skins to reform the government. Rousseau would probably not have written his *Letters* had they been willing to do that. He pointed out that they were not Athenians or Romans but were merchants too occupied with their commercial affairs to pay much attention to government. It was no surprise therefore that they were too distracted to keep their liberty. He seemed to have no illusion that he could rally them through republican shame. I guess we in the modern world are probably more similar to Rousseau's Genevans than to his cherished Romans or Spartans. Why would Tuck think the active citizenship model fits our world?

And there is another issue. I surmised at the start that Tuck's democratic sovereign would make laws either directly by simple majority rule or indirectly through instructions to elected delegates. But the active citizenship ideal would seem to apply to many other settings as well, including the baroque structures of American politics, as far as I can see. If I am a Tuckian agent—who accepts the normative direction to engage actively in making the laws—don't I already have reason to act accordingly, whether or not the institutions of radical democracy are in place? As long as your vote may be sufficient in some voting sequences, Tuck's argument seems to demand this. Is it really the case that, replacing the governmental practices in the United Kingdom with the radical democratic structures Tuck recommends, we would expect an immense increase in agentic behavior?

III

What makes a community's law authoritative on Rousseau's account is the agreement of each person to enter the compact to alienate his or her natural rights for the prospect of something better: "where, unless the election were unanimous, would be the obligation on the minority to submit to the choice of the majority?" (I.5).[14] But why would anyone assent to such an agreement unless each thought it would be, on the whole, in his or her interest? The person must believe ex ante that there are substantial common interests among these people—the prospect of a general will aimed at realizing those interests and a likelihood that it will succeed in realizing those interests. I read this as a condition that might most plausibly apply to a relatively homogeneous community: a small city or farming area, perhaps surrounded by threatening neighbors. As Rousseau commented throughout book II of *The Social Contract* (where he inquires into governments), while larger (and possibly more diverse) communities might rationally be formed, the price would be that the government would have to be small relative to the population: a small aristocratic magistracy or, in the upper limit, a monarchy. Such a government will have a corporate interests (or will) distinct from the general will and will be more easily led to usurp power to its advantage.

I imagine that Geneva might have seemed to Rousseau to have been small enough to govern itself fairly democratically in the early sixteenth century. In any case, that early form of government did not last, as the small council gradually absorbed the powers of the Grand Council and the people lost any role in self-government. Rousseau does not seem to blame increasing diversity or size directly for this evolution. But he does emphasize that as the bourgeoisie became more prosperous, they became distracted by their commercial concerns and lost interest in self-rule. On Rousseau's account, the rights the Genevans lost—to govern themselves—they lost together: they were rights of the majority that had been stolen from them by a small elite. Hence Rousseau's call for the majority to pay attention and take action was plausible when he wrote the *Letters*.

But most modern states are both much larger and much more diverse than Geneva was (even in its mythic past), religiously, ethnically, geographically, and economically. Add to this the various aspects of the information revolutions that spread ideas across borders easily. On Rousseau's account in book II, modern states will tend to run by small governments (relative to their populations) and rely much more on force to back government orders. Such governments will find it easy to take advantage of increasing diversity to target policies to the advantage or disadvantage of specific minorities. Rights lost in complex communities may commonly be lost by minorities—and especially by unpopular or unsympathetic minorities (people accused or convicted of crimes, for example, or racial, ethnic, or religious minorities).

In view of these considerations, one needs to ask this: would people in a large and diverse community be willing rationally to alienate all their rights to a radical democracy? Might they not wish, instead, to insist on some institutional protections against the prospect that any of them could become members of a disfavored minority? Is it really plausible that appeals to the majority, of the sort the one Rousseau urged on the Genevan majority, would be effective in a diverse modern state bent on mistreating criminals, oppressing religious minorities or liberal university professors or other weird people? This is not to deny that majorities can also be oppressed. But as a government needs popular support, that is harder to do. Minorities are vulnerable not only to the government but also to majorities too, and it is hard for me to envision effective remedies for these things in the radical democracy that Tuck hopes to establish.

One response might be to argue that the sovereign, as it is confined to making only general laws that apply equally to everyone, would not be capable of *targeted* oppression. Well, maybe. But what if the forces of oppression or discrimination operate through the economy or the society in some structural way so that they persist unless the government acts remedially? Would general laws be capable of responding to such specific complaints by oppressed minorities? Such responses would have to be particular and targeted, it seems to me, and therefore beyond the powers of the sovereign. The majority could, of course, constitute itself (by law) as a (radical) democracy, and it would then be legally authorized to make particular decrees. But, as we have seen in the United States for the last half century, targeted remedies favoring minorities are often disfavored by majorities. Perhaps the members of the diverse polity will have sufficient virtue to offset this prospect. That seems to ask for a lot of moral self-restraint.

6

Putting Majorities in Their Place

Simone Chambers

DEMOCRACY IS GETTING a serious second look these days. With crisis and backsliding on the horizon, we are reassessing what we value about democracy and where we might have gone wrong in developing its institutions.[1] Professor Richard Tuck's work has long been at the forefront of this critical endeavor, advancing startlingly illuminating rereadings of the founders of our democratic tradition. These Tanner Lectures crystallize many of those earlier insights into a reinvigorated defense of active citizenship embodied in the twin principles of universal suffrage and majority voting.

In defense of his view of active citizenship, Tuck takes issue with the growing interest in sortition as an alternative method of selecting legislators. I begin there. Pushing back against Tuck's skepticism, I defend sortition as a promising tool in what might be called a toolbox of democratic institutions. In the second half of this essay, I connect the toolbox metaphor to a view of democracy, democratic legitimacy, and active citizenship that is very different from Tuck's. The view that I defend does not jettison voting, majorities, and elections, but it does displace voting, majorities, and elections as the exclusive seat of democracy and active citizenship and places them along with sortition in a toolbox.

Sortition

Sortition is a method of choosing members—of an assembly, jury, or committee, for example—by drawing lots or random selection. It was used in ancient Athens and (we think) other Greek democracies to choose executive or agenda-setting assemblies.[2] Every eligible citizen has an equal chance to serve. There are no elections, no campaigning, no money, no parties, no super PACs, no celebrities, no robocalls involved in the selection process. Sortition radically equalizes access to power. Citizens chosen by lot to serve in decision-making institutions are representatives in two senses. The first sense is statistical in that they are a "representative sample" of the general population. This view of representation is often called mirroring. The second view of representation is tied to the task or function a lottocratic assembly might have within a political system. If tasked to make decisions on behalf of the public at large, then the members are supposed to represent the interests of the wider community in their deliberations.

Tuck is right to suggest that right now there is a tremendous amount of interest in sortition within democratic theory.[3] What is the appeal of sortition, and why is it making a comeback now? Tuck suggests four reasons. The first is that many defenders of sortition, like Tuck himself, think that constitutional politics took a wrong turn at the end of the eighteenth century. Tuck's criticism focuses on entrenched rights as replacing the need to call on citizens (Sieyès has much to answer for in this story); these rights and the constitutions that house them are defended as the palladium of each citizen's status as free and equal and as such can replace undependable opinions of real people. Defenders of sortition, by contrast, focus on *electoral* representative government, and the ways it was intentionally designed to exclude ordinary citizens from office and power. Citizens might be equal qua the vote but are not equal qua candidacy for office. This is not a bug but a feature of the eighteenth-century defense of representative government.[4] The unequal access to power has only intensified with the growing inequality of wealth across all constitutional democracies.[5]

Skewed candidacy selection is compounded by a failure of responsiveness. Defenders of sortition often appeal to research that documents a large disconnect between the opinions and interests of lower- and middle-class constituents (indeed the majority) and the policy agendas, endorsements, and voting records of their elected representatives.[6] Even more troubling, this research finds strong correlation between business- and financial-interest lobbying and legislative policy agendas. Thus, low- and middle-income citizens are doubly denied access to power, first through skewed candidate selection and second through a lack of influence over agenda setting.

The second reason Tuck suggests that sortition might be considered attractive is that it offers a mirror view of representation. An assembly chosen through sortition would be a representative sample just like those used in survey research. Indeed, Tuck suggests (perhaps not entirely seriously), why even bring the sample together into an assembly? Why not just use sophisticated sampling techniques to garner public opinion and base policy on that? Although not entirely serious, this suggestion does capture Tuck's central criticism of sortition. It bypasses citizens' agency (no voting, no choice) and ties the democratic credentials of outcomes to their epistemic status as a random sample.

The third and fourth reasons Tuck offers are a fear of majoritarianism and the belief, grounded in rational choice analysis, that individual voting has no impact in any event. I see neither of these reasons present in the literature on sortition. One of the central arguments in favor of sortition is precisely that the majority's needs and interests are ignored by the oligarchs. In the present moment, the turn to sortition is not driven by rational choice assessment of voting but is rather a response to the crisis of representation that sees a dramatic fall in levels of trust in elected representatives because they are out of touch, unresponsive, corrupt, and consumed by partisan reelection concerns rather than the needs of the electorate.

There is a final set of reasons why sortition is garnering so much interest as a democracy-enhancing institutional innovation that Tuck does not canvass. This set of reasons is tied to its track record. For the last thirty years or so, there has been a growing interest in various forms of deliberative democracy, especially the mini public in which sortition is used to choose participants. Mini publics or citizens' assemblies vary in size, structure, and function. But they all have two things in common: (1) they attempt to construct a random (usually stratified) sample of citizens (to counter self-selection, socioeconomic differences, and cultural factors), and (2) they are all structured to promote a certain ideal of deliberation: let's call it nonpartisan evidence-driven debate among equals. Tuck's suggestion that well-designed surveys might be stand-ins for citizens' assemblies fails to acknowledge the importance of deliberation and the second sense of representation I mentioned above. The random selection is the platform for a certain type of impartial deliberation and has little value on its own without that deliberation.

There has been a proliferation of these initiatives across the globe.[7] We have hundreds of well-designed empirical studies measuring and evaluating these initiatives. One of the most common findings is how well ordinary citizens do in these settings.[8] Repeatedly, ordinary citizens show themselves to be competent deliberators able to employ nonpartisan evidence-based reasoning to solve problems.

These initiatives have been largely consultative and not legislative. Quite often they are used to get a sense of what might be called citizens' considered opinions. The outcomes then might inform public debate and policy output. We are seeing larger and larger such groups. In a September 2020 issue of *Science* magazine, for example, there is a call for a global deliberative citizens' assembly on genome editing; France has had a series of such popular gatherings across the country to discuss climate change policy; and the OECD has a recent report endorsing citizen assemblies as an important citizen-centered innovation in democratic governance.

In addition to performing a directly consultative role in policy development, citizens' assemblies and mini publics have been used to inform the public as part of referendum processes. For example, in the Oregon Citizen Initiative Review Boards, citizens chosen at random produce the voter information sheets that go to all registered voters. There is empirical evidence suggesting that citizens at large have higher levels of trust in information and recommendations that come out of randomly selected deliberative forums than from other official sources.[9] In this instance, citizens' assemblies do not replace voters in the process, they replace corrupt stake holders in the process of opinion formation.

The value of and enthusiasm for sortition now is to some extent tied to two features of these deliberative experiments: evidence that ordinary citizens are good and impartial deliberators; and evidence that citizens at large trust the outcomes of these assemblies because the representatives are people like themselves, and they and their deliberations are not exposed to the corrupting forces of electoral politics and money. These successes have contributed to the development of more ambitious uses of sortition—in particular, the idea of using sortition to select a legislative body.

At this point, a randomly selected legislative assembly is purely aspirational. The version of sortition that Tuck challenges in his lectures involves a wildly unrealistic thought experiment in which we are asked to consider replacing elected assemblies with randomly selected ones. Contemplating such a possibility leads Tuck to conclude that "the turn to sortition has patently been a turn away from electoral democracy *as such*, and by playing down the significance of the vote, it leaves the mass of citizens with no *active* role at all; each one *passively* awaits the result of the lottery, in the hope (or maybe the fear) of being called to participate in lawmaking" (chap. 2 sec. II). I want to challenge this assessment on two grounds. First, most work on and endorsement of sortition does not recommend replacing elections with sortition. To date, all citizens' assembly institutional innovations have been introduced to enhance electoral democracy in various ways. Also, within the camp of people who think that a randomly selected legislative assembly might be a good idea, the majority favor introducing it as a second chamber in a bicameral system. On these views, elections and political parties play important roles in democracy (for example, by articulating group interests, developing programmatic policy visions, mobilizing public debate) even if they are open to plutocratic capture. Thus, sortition is introduced as a potential counterbalancing force within the system, not as a replacement for elections. But the bigger issue I want to tackle that is implied by this quote is that voting is the only "active role" that citizens play in a democracy. Instead, I want to defend a view of democracy in which voting is one among many active roles that citizens can play, and the democratic value of voting (and majority rule) is dependent on processes of opinion formation that precede the vote.

Active Citizenship:
Authorization and Collective Action

There are three components to Tuck's picture of active citizenship. The first involves authorization: he says, "laws have no full authority over me—or, to put it another way, that the state is in some sense alien to me—unless I have taken part in making its collective decisions" (chap. 2 sec. III). The second component involves a view of collective action: "the essential characteristic of democratic politics is that the citizens are aware of themselves as engaged in constructing this common activity" (chap. 2 sec. I). I fully embrace these first two components. It is the third move that I find problematic. The third component says that this agentive view is given full and adequate expression in majoritarian voting in which all citizens commit to throwing themselves behind the majoritarian outcome because the majoritarian outcome is the articulation of the collective project. This commitment appears to be independent of either procedural or process issues regarding how the majority came to be the majority or outcome considerations regarding the moral or epistemic substance of the majority outcome.

I think this view gets it wrong. Authorization and a sense of collective democratic agency are tied to the broader context in which votes are taken, especially but not exclusively the context of public debate and opinion formation. This argument will bring me back to sortition and its place within a democratic system.

Voting can involve taking part in a collective process of authorization, but it does not have to. There was a lot of voting in the Supreme Soviet, where legislation regularly received a unanimous show of hands, but there was probably little genuine authorization. Or who knows? We cannot peer into the hearts and minds of the people raising their hands, so instead we rely on procedural clues. Not voting then, but free and fair voting. This suggests that our confidence in voting as an act of a willing agent is primarily accessible via an evaluation of the procedural conditions of voting and not the physical act of casting a ballot or raising a hand.

But Tuck is focused on the immediate moment of voting: "One way of capturing what is implied in the agentive view is precisely that it takes democracy to be in effect a kind of civilized and domesticated version of a mob—and that should not alarm us. Human beings when they gather together physically can effect great changes; . . . The great discovery of democracy was that people could accept a simple head count as the basis for the transformation that they might otherwise have effected through physical action and, potentially, violence" (chap. 2 sec. V). The movement of the mob down the street or the taking part in a vote are, for Tuck, evidence of a common purpose. But what is missing from this account are the conditions under which the mob became a mob, or the majority became the majority. Whether in a mob, in the voting booth, or on the floor of a legislature, if I come to see that I was misled, manipulated, lied to, or denied crucial information, in other words, that I acted in a way that I might not have had I not been manipulated, lied to, or misled, then we can question the grounds for claiming that I authorized the outcome. This in turn suggests that democratic authorization implies a robust view of the conditions of opinion and will formation. This is one reason why we are so concerned with present levels of misinformation. Misinformation and propaganda are endemic to all democratic public spheres, but we appear to be coming close to a tipping point where some very basic conditions of democratic authorization are in jeopardy.

Tuck resists such procedural conditions and insists that guaranteeing universal suffrage is all the safeguard we need. "Most clear cases of so-called illiberal democracy in fact involve taking the vote away from minorities, either formally, through denying them citizenship, or informally, through corruption of the voting process" (chap. 2 sec. IV). This view misjudges illiberal democracies. Regimes like Hungary and Turkey that find themselves sliding ever more deeply into authoritarianism do not attack elections or voting. On the contrary, they are continually holding up their regimes as bastions of democracy precisely because they rely on majoritarian support. Instead, they attack and undermine the public sphere by silencing opposition voices, flooding the digital airwaves with falsehood and confusion, and branding criticism and debate obstacles to the will of the people.[10] These autocrats can see very well that it is information, criticism, and open debate that are the real enemies of authoritarianism, not universal suffrage. And this makes them enemies of democracy, not just of liberalism.

Closer to home, there are active attempts in the United States to "corrupt the vote process." Some of those are frontal attacks on the franchise by, for example, purging voter rolls, making it difficult and onerous to vote, and most recently attempting to have legitimate ballots thrown out or go uncounted. But most of the damage done to the integrity of voting is done through misinformation and disinformation mediated by the public sphere. Voter suppression and election challenge are carried forward on a mendacious public narrative claiming voter fraud where there is none. Millions of Americans believe that the 2020 election was stolen when there is clear evidence that it was not. This belief is the direct result of an elite-driven misinformation campaign[11] that will do more damage to our democratic system than any questionable and partisan demand for voter ID laws or stricter absentee ballot rules. In mass democracies the "voting process" is highly dependent on and mediated by the public sphere. Enemies of democracy know this and so set out to wreck the public sphere and manipulate public opinion rather than directly disenfranchise people.[12] The "taking part" that can authorize law cannot be fully captured in the simple act of voting but must also involve procedural safeguards that help ensure some level of autonomy for the agents involved, especially in processes of opinion formation.

Active citizenship, for Tuck, is not just about voting but voting together. Like the view of authorship analogized as a mob moving together, collective action is understood in terms of doing, not thinking. Rousseau captures this sentiment in a startling passage that Tuck quotes approvingly (twice) in the lectures: "it is less a question of deliberation here than of concord; the choice of which course you will take is not the greatest question: Were it bad in itself, take it all together; by that alone it will become the best" (chap. 2 sec. I). On this view, the minority is swept along with the majority and enfolded into the collective action. Citizens are said to commit to majority rule not simply in the sense that they abide by the outcomes but in a deeper sense that, once outvoted, they take the majority view to be their view: "as a democrat, I agree that once the majority view is known, I accept it as my own" (chap. 2 sec. V). After a vote, the minority disappears and outcomes are as if passed and authorized unanimously: "the actual implementation of a vote by an assembly is unanimous; at the point at which (for example) the resolution of an assembly becomes a law, there *is* no minority" (ibid.). I find this an unpersuasive account of the legitimacy of majority rule and an implausible account of why minorities go along with majority decisions.

An alternative defense of majority rule is precisely that it ensures that minority views do not disappear. With majority rule we have a public record that reflects that there were other reasons and arguments that were persuasive even if they did not win the day. Bernard Manin (among others) is a defender of this view: "The process (majority voting) nevertheless institutionalizes the admission that there were also reasons not to desire the solution finally adopted."[13] Majority rule makes the minority visible in a way that consensus, unanimity, or supermajority rules do not.[14] The visibility of the minority means that those in power need to justify their actions to the minority as well. Majorities elect governments but governments govern everybody, and therefore their reasons and justifications must address everybody. On Tuck's account, minority opposition and dissent simply disappear and require no further thought on the part of the winners.

This alternative way of justifying majority rule ties it to public debates and deliberative accountability; it ties it to processes whereby the majority came to be the majority. Deliberation in which the minority feels like their case was addressed and honestly considered is one of the strongest defenses of majority voting. It is famously defended by John Dewey: "majority rule, just as majority rule, is as foolish as its critics charge it with. But it never is *merely* majority rule . . . antecedent debates, modification of views to meet the opinions of minorities, the relative satisfaction given the latter by the fact that it has had a chance and that next time it may be successful in becoming a majority. . . . The essential need, in other words, is the improvement of the methods and conditions of debate, discussion and persuasion."[15] To illustrate this view, I want to end with a brief comparison of three recent constitutional referendums and the public processes that preceded the votes.

Both Ireland and the United Kingdom used referendums to decide divisive and polarizing issues of constitutional change. In Ireland, citizens voted on gay marriage and abortion in 2015 and 2018, respectively, while in the United Kingdom the question of exit from the European Union (Brexit) was voted on in 2016. I want to suggest that the Irish process was relatively successful as an exercise in collective democratic action while the Brexit case was not. The success of the former can be linked to the initiation of a productive national conversation over time, in which sectarian and partisan divisions were channeled into hard-fought but generally civil debates not derailed by misinformation. In both Irish referendums, the questions were formulated and deliberated by a randomly selected citizens' assembly. This inserted an impartial public player into the process that functioned to build trust and facilitate public debate.[16] That public debate saw many civil society organizations, from churches to local book clubs, hosting discussion and debate at a grassroots level. Although the referendum votes were a decisive moment, the processes involved the triangulation between three democratic institutions—Parliament, a citizens' assembly, and a referendum—and a concerted effort to engage active citizen participation in a drawn-out public debate. This is what I call a toolbox approach to democratic self-government. Multiple institutions are deployed in order to create a legitimate and fair democratic process that can facilitate collective problem solving; honor and respect differences of opinion, including minority views; and produce an outcome that is decisive and stable and one that citizens can take ownership of. The process is designed so that the moment of voting, the moment that is so important for Tuck, really does reflect a collective action that even the losers think was fair and gave them a chance to make their case.

The Brexit story is very different. Whereas in Ireland it appears that real thought went into designing a process that would facilitate a national conversation, the Brexit referendum was a comparatively rushed affair focused more on the vote than on the preceding process. The poor quality of public deliberation, widespread misinformation, debilitating polarization, and a referendum question that skated above and obscured the how, when, what, and who issues involved in leaving the EU, produced a process, the legitimacy of which is still in dispute. The minority who lost the vote are not throwing their lot in with the majority and acting as if the vote were unanimous. And this I would contend is not because they have misunderstood the meaning of majority rule; it is because they question whether the referendum vote was an expression of an authentic collective agency.

This brief comparison is only meant to suggest that majority voting and universal suffrage alone cannot capture democratic authorship or, to use Tuck's words, citizens' awareness "of themselves as engaged in constructing this common activity," which is "the essential characteristic of democratic politics" (chap. 2 sec. I).

Conclusion

In the complex relationship between democratic citizenship at large and the state, voting is only one way citizens play an active role and demand effective responsiveness and accountability. Citizens challenging state actors through the courts; a critical and free press that asks hard questions; an active civil society that can organize and identify salient issues; street politics and protests that channel, articulate, and publicize grievances and injustice; innovative and effective forms of citizen consultation at all levels of government (randomly selected citizens' assemblies for example)—these are just some of the ways that citizens exercise constraint on and demand responsiveness from the state. These are some of the ways that citizens are, and can think of themselves as, authors and agents of change.

Democracy is a system in which the active agent of democratic self-determination should not be identified with any empirical majority. Instead, we should seek that agent in a set of disaggregated and decentered procedures, processes, and institutions over time, punctuated, to be sure, by elections and majority-rule decisions. Universal suffrage is a necessary but not sufficient condition of legitimacy because only a system where voices as well as votes have power to influence and determine decisions can live up to ideals of democracy. This view is sometimes called a post-sovereignty view, as it rejects the classic view (found in Hobbes and Rousseau but also in Schmitt) of sovereignty as indivisible and irresistible, sovereignty as a big buck stopper. Instead, sovereignty is measured along a number of institutional and social measures that produce the procedural potential of both unmanipulated and reasonable opinion formation on the input side and differentiated responsiveness and accountability on the output side. But I would prefer to retain the phrase "popular sovereignty" and try to give it a different meaning than Rousseau, a meaning that can accommodate the equality of all citizens and radical pluralism, that does not efface minority voices, and that recognizes the assault on democratic agency posed by misinformation, propaganda, and manipulation.

Response

7

Reply to Commentators

I

I would like to begin my response to the commentators by expressing heartfelt thanks to them all. Their presence at the lectures, and the developed comments which they have contributed to this volume, made the occasion both intellectually stimulating and greatly enjoyable—a model of academic debate.

Despite the many differences between them, there are, I think, two main themes that can be discerned in what they say. One is that Rousseau did not mean what I ascribe to him—that he could not have been the kind of ultra-radical majoritarian that I claim he had been. The second—and it is related—is that ultra-radical majoritarianism is self-evidently a highly dangerous principle, and that is why we should not suppose Rousseau to have espoused it, at least if we are to continue to take him seriously as an important political theorist. (Schwartzberg, it should be said, would not join in this condemnation of majoritarianism, unlike the other commentators; but also unlike me, she believes that Rousseau was not majoritarian enough.) I will deal with the first issue, the interpretation of Rousseau, first and then turn to the second issue, the question of what the kind of theory I have attributed to Rousseau would mean in a modern state, and whether we should fear it.

As someone said during our conversations after the lectures, Rousseau's writings are like the famous duck-rabbit optical puzzle, which looked at one way is a duck, and another way is a rabbit, without any change in the picture itself. From quite an early period in the reading of Rousseau, he came to be seen either as a radical majoritarian democrat or as a kind of modern liberal, and his texts seemed to support either interpretation, depending on the assumptions of the reader. In this situation, I have found it helpful to reflect on how Rousseau placed himself in the debates over politics in his own time, and how as a consequence he was judged by his contemporaries. I would not make any more far-reaching claims for this approach than that it is helpful in steering us in one direction when faced by a problem of this kind: there are many different ways of reading texts, and they all have something to be said for them. But it does at the very least place a burden on those who want to read Rousseau in a way that does not correspond to his known position in those debates.

It has often seemed to me that Rousseau is best understood through his hatreds—and he was undeniably a very good hater. In the case of his political theory, it is clear whom he hated: it was the writers on "modern" natural law whose works dominated the intellectual life of the mid-eighteenth century, in particular Grotius, Pufendorf, Barbeyrac, and their popularizer Burlamaqui; it is worth observing that these were the same authors whom Kant despised as "sorry comforters" for drawing the principles of international law from their own philosophical reasoning.[1] In Barbeyrac's great editions of Grotius and Pufendorf, and in their translations, eighteenth-century readers found a complete encyclopedia of modern political theory, which they seldom needed to supplement with any other works; it would have been this edition of Grotius that Rousseau described as lying on his father's workbench. And in that encyclopedia, the constant argument was that human beings are naturally sociable, albeit to a limited degree (that is, not to the degree that Aristotle had supposed, Aristotelianism being something they all rejected). Humans in principle might, as a consequence, be able to live without states, but in practice they usually required a system of common security to protect the interests that they shared, and so they created political institutions. All these writers to a greater or lesser extent also believed that the creation of states was a two-stage process, involving two "contracts." The first was an agreement to live a common life together, and the second was an agreement to create a particular kind of government (usually, from the point of view of eighteenth-century Europe, a liberal monarchy).

The doctrines of human sociability and the double contract were presented by Pufendorf, Barbeyrac, and Burlamaqui quite straightforwardly as repudiations of Hobbes. The doctrines were connected, since (as these authors observed) Hobbes had expressly denied that human beings could securely align any of their beliefs or interests; they might by doing so create an adventitious "concord" or *consensio*, but because of the deep and far-reaching character of human disagreement, the only means to such an alignment was what he called "union" or *unio*, that is, the wholesale subordination of their judgment in all matters (other than those to do with bare survival) to a common judge. No sociable life was possible without this subordination, and no agreement could take place before a "contract" to create the common judge, that is, a sovereign. Hobbes was quite open about the extreme character of his theory, asserting in a remarkable passage at the end of his *Elements of Law* that

> the civil laws are to all subjects the measures of their actions, whereby to determine, whether they be right or wrong, profitable or unprofitable, virtuous or vicious; and by them the use and definition of all names not agreed upon, and tending to controversy, shall be established. As for example, upon the occasion of some strange and deformed birth, it shall not be decided by Aristotle, or the philosophers, whether the same be a man or no, but by the laws. (II.10.8)

Though the second part of the *Elements* was not available in a foreign language until 1772, similar claims can be found in *De Cive*. For example:

> suppose a woman gives birth to a deformed figure, and the law forbids killing a human being, the question arises whether the new-born is a human being. The question then is, what is a human being? No one doubts that the commonwealth will decide—and without taking account of the Aristotelian definition, that a Man is a rational Animal. (XVII.12)

And

> if, notwithstanding the law of nature's prohibition of theft, adultery etc.,[2] the civil law commands such an infringement, the act does not count as theft, adultery etc. When in the old days the Lacedaemonians gave permission to boys by a specific enactment to pilfer other people's things, they laid it down that those things were not other people's but belonged to the pilferer; and so such pilferings were not thefts; similarly among the pagans sexual relationships were by their laws legal marriages. (XIV.10)

Moreover, in *De Cive*, which (we should never forget) was the most widely read of his works on the Continent,[3] Hobbes was explicit that the contract that created a civil society had initially to be *democratic*:

> When men have met to erect a commonwealth, they are, almost by the very fact that they have met, a *Democracy*. From the fact that they have gathered voluntarily, they are understood to be bound by the decisions made by agreement of the majority. And that is a *Democracy*, as long as the convention lasts, or is set to reconvene at certain times and places. For a convention whose will is the will of all the citizens has *sovereign power*. And because it is assumed that each man in this convention has the right to vote, it follows that it is a *Democracy*. (VII.5)[4]

And in this chapter VII of *De Cive*, he provided what before Rousseau was—astonishingly enough—the most systematic discussion available in post-classical literature of democracy and majority voting, including a long account of the distinction between sovereignty (*imperium*) and government (*administratio*) which, as I showed in my Seeley Lectures, must have been in part the inspiration for Rousseau's similar distinction. Pufendorf and the others were well aware of the democratic implications of Hobbes's ideas, at least as expressed in *De Cive*; Pufendorf described them as "highly dangerous and prejudicial to all those limited Princes, who are ordain'd by the voluntary Donation of the People, and bound up to certain fundamental Laws," since on Hobbes's account those princes were the servants of a democratic sovereign.[5] His own emphasis on the need for two contracts was principally designed to undermine the idea of the primary democracy, and to show that people could go straight to monarchy without any prior act of majority voting, though he was unable to explain how the initial assembly made its decision about the form of government without some kind of vote.

Rousseau made very clear in his writings how he placed himself in this argument between Hobbes and his critics, and his own contempt for the "modern natural law" school.[6] As he said in the Second Discourse, "all the rules of natural right" can be derived "without it being necessary to introduce [the principle] of sociability," a remark that to his contemporary readers unequivocally aligned him with Hobbes.[7] As for the double contract, he was equally clear, saying in *The Social Contract* (III.6) that "There is only one contract in the State, and that is the act of association, which in itself excludes the existence of a second."[8] He drew the same conclusions from these principles as Hobbes, and indeed quoted him (without acknowledgment) in his *Political Economy* when he said that the

> general will, which tends always to the preservation and welfare of the whole and of every part, and is the source of the laws, constitutes for all the members of the State, in their relations to one another and to it, the rule of what is just or unjust: a truth which shows, by the way, how idly some writers have treated as theft the subtlety prescribed to children at Sparta for obtaining their frugal repasts, as if everything ordained by the law were not lawful.[9]

As I wrote in chapters 1 and 2, we should not underestimate the extremism of the position Rousseau was endorsing—the same extremism of which Hobbes was accused by Rousseau's contemporaries. After all, he made it entirely explicit in the letter to Mirabeau, which I quoted in extenso but which unfortunately none of my commentators refer to. If finding "*a form of Government that might place the law above man*" is like squaring the circle, something Rousseau believed to be impossible, then

> one has to go to the other extreme and all at once place man as much above the law as he can be, consequently to establish a despotism that is arbitrary and indeed the most arbitrary possible: I would wish the despot could be God. In a word, I see no mean between

the most austere Democracy and the most perfect Hobbesism: for the conflict between men and the laws, which makes for a perpetual intestine war in the State, is the worst of all political States.

"Hobbesism," here, means autocratic monarchy—although eighteenth-century readers were aware of the role of democracy in Hobbes's thought, partly via Pufendorf, they also always saw him as ultimately a theorist of absolutist monarchy, and Rousseau was no different, despite his obvious debt to the discussion of democracy in *De Cive*. But there can be no doubt that in this letter Rousseau signaled that his "most austere Democracy" would be a *Hobbesian* democracy, an arbitrary despotism. Looking back in book IX of his *Confessions*, he recalled that after his time in Venice in 1743/44, "my views had become much more extended by the historical study of morality. I had perceived everything to be radically connected with politics [*tout tenoit radicalement à la politique*]," and it was this conviction—that politics is at the base of morality and not vice versa—that animated all his writings on the subject.

II

Given this background, let us consider the alternative readings of Rousseau that some of my commentators put forward. The most important of these interpretations comes, unsurprisingly, from Josh Cohen, who has thought long and hard about Rousseau's texts, and from whom I differed with some trepidation. Cohen sums up his view in the following passage:

> A society under the supreme direction of the general will is a form of association in which citizens share a conception of their common interests or "common good," use that shared understanding as the basis for their political judgments, and treat those political judgments as having priority over judgments about how best to advance their own particular interests.

As he says, this is a summary of the argument he put forward in his 2010 book *Rousseau: A Free Community of Equals*, where he said (for example) that Rousseau's theory

requires that individuals commit to regarding themselves as be-
longing to a political community whose members are committed
to regarding one another as equals: ackowledging one another as
political equals, with equal status in establishing the laws; recog-
nizing one another as equally subject to the laws by reference to
reasons of the common good, which give equal weight to the good
of each citizen. Moreover, Rousseau proposes to institutionalize
the general will's supremacy through a direct democracy, whose
equal citizens regularly assemble to reaffirm their social bonds and
decide on the fundamental laws best suited to advancing the common good, and in which limits on social-economic inequality help
to sustain the institutions. (15–16)

Much of this I would agree with: there is no doubt that *equality* is
at the heart of Rousseau's ideas, though that would not differentiate
him from Hobbes, who remarked in the *Elements of Law* that "equality is the law of nature" (I.17.4) and who stressed both there and in
De Cive the obligation on men both in nature and in civil society to
think of themselves as equal with one another.[10] Where we disagree,
I think, is over the character of what Cohen calls a shared conception
of the common good. To put the disagreement in terms that would
have been recognizable in the eighteenth century: is this shared conception *consensio*, consensus, or is it *unio*, union? In other words, is it
something that in principle and possibly even in practice can be prior
to or independent of the *political* process that produces a general
will? Or is it the *product* of that process, and if so, how? If it is the
former, then it is fundamentally the theory of Pufendorf and the other
jurisconsultes, and if the latter, it is equally fundamentally the theory
of Hobbes and—I would say—Rousseau.

In his book, Cohen is unequivocal in his answer to this question:
there has to be a consensus (a term he actually uses, as it happens) of
a reasonably substantive kind before there can be a general will.[11]
There will be scope for what he calls "reasonable disagreements,"
but there will have to be an (undefined) zone of agreement on what
will constitute a common good before—if we are to be concrete—
the citizens go into the assembly to vote on laws. On Cohen's view, a
democratic state is extremely useful at securing this common good;

it may even be practically necessary in any sublunary world with which we are familiar; but in theory there could be a consensus robust enough to sustain many social practices without recourse to voting and legislation. This seems like modern common sense, but that common sense is to an extent the product of a reaction to a very different view, captured in Kant's remark quoted above that "so far, no one has fully understood that it is one of the first duties to enter civil society. Hobbes and Rousseau, however, have had some idea of this"—and Kant himself, he believed, had fully thought this through.[12] On this view, collective human action requires something like a state ("civil society" in Kant and his predecessors meaning a state, of course). Without a state or a sovereign, we not only have no physical security, we have no what we might call "epistemic security"—a set of agreed judgments about the world and human life on which we can converge in order to be able to act together.

According to Rousseau, at least in his writings on politics, we bring very little into the social contract—natural man is governed by *amour de soi* and *pitié*, but *amour de soi* is essentially the desire for self-preservation, and *pitié* is no basis for reciprocal relations between human beings, since it is the instinctive revulsion at misfortune or cruelty that we feel for all living creatures.[13] He spelled this out in a passage in the manuscript for *Social Contract*, which, although it did not make it into the final version (which is itself far from being a fully completed work), captures his fundamental idea.

[T]he Law is anterior to justice and not the other way round. And if the Law cannot be unjust, it is not because justice is its basis (which is not necessarily the case) but because it is against nature for one to wish to harm oneself. To this there are no exceptions.

It is a beautiful and sublime precept to do unto others as we would be done unto. But is it not evident that, far from serving as the foundation of justice, it itself needs a foundation? For what clear and solid reason have I for behaving, being myself, according to the will I would have if I were somebody else?[14] It is also clear that this precept is subject to a thousand exceptions which have never been explained except by sophistry. Would not a judge who condemns a criminal wish to be pardoned if he was a criminal himself?

Where is the man who would ever wish to be refused anything? Does it follow that we should be granted everything we ask? This other axiom, *cuique suum*, on which all right of property is based, what foundation has it other than the right of property itself? And if I do not say, with Hobbes, "everything is mine," why should I not at least recognize as mine, in the state of nature, everything which is useful to me and of which I gain possession?[15]

The need to cooperate, in the face of natural disasters and human aggression, requires us (Rousseau thought) to become different kinds of creatures and to submit our individual judgments to a collective judgment. It was their awareness of the alarming character of this claim that led his contemporaries to attack him, just as it had been their awareness of the similarly alarming claim that Hobbes had made that led them to attack him. But both Hobbes and Rousseau threw down a challenge: politics is potentially and at its best a transparent and organized way of controlling our common life. In its absence, more insidious means of exercising power are given free rein—what we would term "cultural" power, and which they often treated as the power of rhetoricians. The hatred that Hobbes expressed for lawyers, priests, and scientists,[16] and Rousseau for "the professors,"[17] was hatred for the exercise of this kind of power, and they thought that only a well-constituted state with very far-reaching capacities could protect us from it.

Majoritarianism, for both of them, I think, was important because it was a procedure that made as small a claim as possible to any authority beyond the purely political. It was not the substantive rectitude of the outcome, but solely the numbers of people supporting it, that made it authoritative. Rousseau, I believe, would have been startled by the epistemic interpretation of the general will, since it makes the point of majoritarianism its efficacy at finding some independently specifiable "correct" or "best" solution to a political problem, and the whole point of this approach to politics is to deny that there *is* such a solution. This seems to me the plain reading of the passage at the end of *Letters Written from the Mountain* that I quoted in chapter 1: "Were it bad in itself, take it all together; by that alone it will become the best." Cohen acknowledges the difficulty of this passage but argues that taking something "together" (on his interpretation of Rousseau) implies a more complex and substantive set of commitments than I believe to be the case. But Rousseau on Cohen's account is still left saying that a measure can be "bad in itself" and is only made good by the unanimity with which it is passed, and it is hard to make sense of this if Rousseau thought that the process of collective decision *picks out* good outcomes, rather than *constitutes* them.

The hostility of both Hobbes and Rousseau to deliberative democracy was part of their anxiety over the power of oratory and persuasion, and, as we saw, it was at the heart of Sieyès's critique of Rousseauism:

> It is not in the watches of the night, with everyone in their own houses, that the democrats who are most jealous of their liberty form and fix their individual opinion, to be carried from there into the public space; only to return to their houses to start over again in complete solitude, in the event that no will common to the majority could be extracted from these isolated opinions.[18]

But Sieyès's mockery should not blind us to the fact that something like this was what Rousseau believed, though with qualifications. I quoted Rousseau's famous remark in book II chapter 3 that "[i]f, when the people, being furnished with adequate information, held its deliberations, the citizens had no communication one with another, the grand total of the small differences would always give the general will," but I could also have quoted a passage from book IV chapter 1:

> I could here set down many reflections on the simple right of voting in every act of Sovereignty—a right which no-one can take from the citizens—and also on the right of stating views, making proposals, dividing and discussing, which the government is always most careful to leave solely to its members; but this important subject would need a treatise to itself.

Although Cohen in his book said of this passage that "there is no suggestion here that the government is right to confine discussion in these ways" (p. 77), there is also no suggestion in this chapter, which deals with the "indestructibility" of the general will, that Rousseau is being at all ironic, and that we should not take what he says at face value. We must remember the point I made in chapter 1, and in my book *The Sleeping Sovereign*, that Rousseau always assumes a sharp distinction between sovereignty and government; he indeed described the distinction as the key to understanding democratic politics.[19] The democratic sovereign rules on the fundamental laws—we might say the constitution—but not on other political questions; those are left to a government which Rousseau thought should *not* be a straightforward democracy. Many readers of Rousseau assume that this "government" is simply an executive implementing the laws and applying them to particular cases, but that (I argued in *The Sleeping Sovereign*) is to misunderstand Rousseau's distinction.

If we take the American political system as an example, the sovereign, for Rousseau, would be the people voting on their constitution, and the government would be the structure created by the Constitution, made up of the Congress, Presidency, and Supreme Court. This indeed is how many of the American founders theorized what they were doing.[20] It would also correspond to what Rousseau said about the desirability of a mixed government (III.7). In some sense the American government, broadly defined, applies the laws of the Constitution to particular cases, but it does a lot more, including debating measures in representative deliberative assemblies. What Rousseau seems to have thought is that such assemblies present no dangers if they are clearly subordinate to the will of the sovereign, but the sovereign's will cannot itself be expressed in such a setting without running the risk of distortion through oratorical skill and the inherent problems created by systems of representation; in our terms, he wanted plebiscites or effective mandation from popular assemblies to supply the fundamental rules of a civil society. Hobbes, it should be said, was also in fact not against deliberation if it could be hived off into an assembly that did not possess ultimate legislative power.[21]

The question of how this protection from the orators, or from cultural power, can be managed in a modern society with mass media is, of course, one that has troubled many political theorists; but one way of thinking about it is to stress that for Hobbes and Rousseau, the dangerous form that the power of the orators took was *partial association*: the creation of political parties that would inevitably distort the votes of their members. As I wrote in chapter 1, in virtually every passage where Rousseau talks about the general will ceasing to be general, he links this solely to the appearance of partial associations and not to any cognitive or moral failure on the part of the citizens. It may be that if these kinds of association can be avoided, and if the votes of the citizens are on single issues that do not require party loyalty (as in a modern constitutional referendum), something of his idea can be preserved in the very different conditions of a modern state.

In her dazzling response to my book *The Sleeping Sovereign*,[22] Melissa Schwartzberg made the telling point that I was being too parsimonious in my analysis of the sovereign/government distinction: should a Rousseauian not push for as wide a use of sovereignty as possible, rather than limit it to what we customarily think of as constitutional matters? Were the Jacobins not as much Rousseauian as the Girondins (something I had denied in the book)? I have come to think that there is much in what she said, but the question is in the end a pragmatic one. Rousseau thought that in a modern society, it was unlikely that citizens would have a great deal of time for the kind of democratic assemblies he envisaged, and that a form of representation would therefore be necessary; as he said, addressing the citizens of Geneva in the Eighth Letter from the Mountain:

> Not being idle as ancient Peoples were, you cannot ceaselessly occupy yourselves with the Government as they did: but by that very fact that you can less constantly keep watch over it, it should be instituted in such a way that it might be easier for you to see its intrigues and provide for abuses. Every public effort that your interest demands ought to be made all the easier for you to fulfill since it is an effort that costs you and that you do not make willingly.[23]

If it is in practice possible for modern citizens genuinely to take part in well-ordered collective decisions about their common life more often than the twice-yearly meetings in the Cathedral of the Genevan General Council, which Rousseau had in mind,[24] then they should do so; the problem with the Jacobins (the Girondins thought) was that only the Parisian mob would actually influence political discussions, given the vastness and complexity of France. In our societies, however, even strictly constitutional questions are scarcely ever revisited in most people's lifetimes, let alone twice a year! To get back to something of the sort which Rousseau envisaged would be quite an achievement in itself.

III

Cohen is sympathetic to Rousseau's political vision but thinks I have misunderstood it and turned it into something that is unacceptable. Schwartzberg also thinks I have misunderstood Rousseau, but her sympathies are the other way around from Cohen's: she finds my own ideas appealing but dislikes what she takes to have been Rousseau's own views. Ferejohn, too, thinks I have omitted important and potentially distasteful features of Rousseau's theory; in particular, both Schwartzberg and Ferejohn are anxious about the restrictions that (they argue) Rousseau in fact places on his citizenry.

Schwartzberg's criticisms focus on two things. One is my—admittedly rather reckless—claim that Rousseau would not necessarily have supposed that women were excluded from the ranks of citizens; she thinks that Sieyès, despite the fact that he placed women among the "passive" citizens, did so only provisionally, and that a Sieyèsian politics might in principle be more egalitarian than a Rousseauian one. Like most people who have written about Rousseau's misogyny—or at least his belief that women must have a different social role from that of men—she leans most heavily on *Emile*, where Rousseau expressly addresses the question. The relationship between *Emile* and Rousseau's directly political works (that is, the writings that grew out of his *Political Institutions* project, particularly the Second Discourse, *The Social Contract*, the article on economy, and his draft essays on international relations) is a notoriously difficult one to analyze; I referred above to the question of "benign" *amour propre*, where the ideas in *Emile* seem almost in direct contradiction to those in the Second Discourse. It is also the case that even taken by itself, *Emile* can be ambiguous; what are we to make, for example, of its sequel, which Rousseau left unfinished but whose plot we know, in which the entire relationship between Emile and Sophie falls apart, and the teachings of the tutor seem to be undermined by the eventual fate of the two protagonists? Sophie is unfaithful but takes on the full responsibility of educating her child by Emile; Emile abandons both her and the child and becomes (for a time) a slave. Most commentators on this work (and they are increasing in number) have taken it at the very least to call into question what the tutor says and does in educating both Emile and Sophie. My thought in chapter 1 was that we should treat the works that sprang from *Political Institutions* as freestanding and concerned with a rather general set of questions, and that we should not necessarily read into them what we think Rousseau was saying in his other works, especially those that are explicitly fictional. Great literary art is a complex thing. I also thought that the actual role of women in eighteenth-century politics across Europe is widely misunderstood, and that to deny them a role would in fact have been more innovatory than giving them one—an innovation that Rousseau strikingly did *not* make when outlining a constitution for Corsica. Perhaps we should give Rousseau the benefit of the doubt in this respect.

Schwartzberg has another basis for her belief that Sieyès is a better model than Rousseau for the ideas I put forward in the second chapter. This is the conviction (which she shares with Cohen) that the passages in which Rousseau talks about the characteristics of the general will not being present in the majority (notably the famous passage in *The Social Contract* IV.2) imply something about a "demanding" moral character that is required of citizens. Sieyès, on her account, is not at all demanding in this way, and is in fact closer to being a simple majoritarian of the kind I want. (Cohen, while thinking the same as Schwartzberg about these passages, seems on the other hand rather to welcome their demanding quality.) But as I said in my discussion of Rousseau, the point of IV.2 is quite clearly simply to justify majority rule: "the vote of the majority always binds all the rest. This follows from the contract itself. But it is asked how a man can be both free and forced to conform to wills that are not his own. How are the opponents at once free and subject to laws they have not agreed to?" And as I said, this is in effect Wollheim's "paradox of democracy," and Rousseau's reply to his own question says nothing about the attitudes or beliefs of the citizen. His answer was a rather dramatic way of putting the thought that my vote (as Harrison observed a propos of Wollheim) is in a way provisional: I will correct it in the light of what my fellow citizens vote for, since my overriding commitment is to align my will with that of the majority, irrespective of the *content* of the majority will. Otherwise I am left merely feeling dominated by some of my fellow citizens, and this above all is what Rousseau wishes us to avoid.

The problem with Sieyès as a model, from my point of view, and this needs reiterating against Schwartzberg, is his insistence on the necessity of what we might call "free" representation, representation without mandation, at all levels. Passivity and this kind of representation go together; such representation is always a *pis aller*, pragmatically necessary but undeniably exclusionary in its effects—as Schwartzberg herself argued in her review of *The Sleeping Sovereign*. As I said, on Sieyès's account, even the "active" citizens are in the end not much less "passive" than the others.

IV

Ferejohn, too, thinks that Rousseau required a great deal of his citizens, and that this makes his theory potentially highly illiberal. He is particularly concerned with the implications of a Rousseauian theory of the kind I endorse for immigration.

> Presumably the state must have the authority to restrict entry to assure that those who enter are suitably committed to common purposes. This may be a very demanding and potentially quite illiberal requirement. Potential entrants might need to show they are morally worthy of citizenship. . . . Moreover, is state policy to be restricted only to admitting (some of) those people who appear to be committed to active citizenship of the kind Tuck recommends? Or may the failure to conform to the morality of active citizenship also justify expulsions of those already in the community?

But this is very far from what I believe (and, I would like to suppose, what Rousseau also thought). As I said in response to Schwartzberg, it is a key part of my argument that Rousseau did *not* think that his citizens had to commit themselves to anything more than accepting the result of a majority vote. If I am right that it is the result of the vote that *constitutes* their "common purpose," then the only necessary condition to impose upon immigrants is that they are willing to be citizens of a majoritarian democracy. Whether that is sufficient is another matter: as I said at the end of the second chapter, the principle that all residents must be treated as citizens seems to me to imply that there must be some kind of immigration policy, but what it should be, and how extensive it should be, is entirely a matter for the existing citizens.

But it should be said that anything like a "moral" requirement would run entirely counter to the spirit of a Rousseauian or a radical democracy, since such a requirement implies that there is something other than the bare fact of participating in majority voting that makes someone a democratic citizen. The same is true of any cultural requirement; as I remarked in my second chapter, "the emphasis on *national* identity as it developed in the nineteenth century was inherently *anti-democratic*, since it required something other than the activity of democracy to be what united citizens, and by doing so it devalued active politics altogether." If this is true for immigration, then it also rules out Ferejohn's fear of expelling existing citizens—unless that is a variant on the general fear of majoritarian oppression, to which I shall turn presently. Ferejohn points to Rousseau's willingness to countenance for a time the continued existence of serfdom in Poland, and his similar willingness to support the rebellion of the slave owners in British North America, as evidence for the limits on his democratic commitments; but it is clear that in both cases, this was for Rousseau a matter of practical politics—just as the denial of the franchise to women was for Bentham and (if Schwartzberg is right) for Sieyès. It would be a mistake to deny Bentham's obvious and repeated support for female suffrage on the grounds that he did not suppose it could be immediately implemented in Britain, though it could be in Revolutionary France, and it would be the same mistake to turn Rousseau's remarks about Poland and America against him.

Ferejohn also argues that I must be wrong in supposing that a law has authority over me as long as I have taken part in making it, even if I was outvoted, on the grounds that this is potentially "anarchism": if I choose not to vote, he thinks, I can deny the authority of the result. But abstention (in most voting systems) on the part of the member of an assembly or of a committee is treated as a *vote*—I am still a member of the assembly and committed to its decisions even if I abstain, and I do not see why this is not true if I am a democratic citizen. The heart of my argument is that there need be no difference in principle between being a member of a democratic assembly and being the citizen of a mass democracy. Whether I formally abstain, or am taken to be abstaining by virtue of my inaction, is then a relatively minor matter; countries where voting is compulsory, such as Australia, leave an option for abstention—in Australia (as I understand it) one can simply submit a blank ballot form—but abstention in other countries is signalled by not turning up.

V

The one commentator who comprehensively dissents from the views I put forward in the lectures is Chambers. She provides a sturdy defense of exactly the approach to democracy that I have been questioning. She is also more concerned with the problems of democracy in modern states than the other commentators, though assumptions about these problems underlie much of what they too say. What she urges is that we should think of democracy as offering a complex and varied set of institutions in which citizens can take part and have some influence on the terms of their common life; voting is one of those institutions, but it should not dominate the political arena to the exclusion of all others. She points us towards "authoritarian" regimes such as Hungary and Turkey, which (she says) have characteristically not sought to undermine voting but have tried to restrict other aspects of citizens' political life. And she defends sortition as a way of representing citizens' opinions without the corrupting effect of modern party politics and mass media—though she shies away from thinking that this should imply its use in a much wider range of settings than the "citizen juries" that are becoming commonplace. It is in her comments that we see most clearly the fear of majoritarianism that I mentioned at the beginning of this response, and to which I will now turn.

The apprehensions expressed by Chambers, and shared by many of our contemporaries (with the notable exception among the commentators of Schwartzberg), derive, I believe, from two sources. The first is the general anxiety about what is sometimes called "authoritarian populism"; Chambers's examples, as I said, are modern Hungary and Turkey, but the template (so to speak) for this idea goes back first to the Terror of 1793/94 and was then refashioned to fit what we might call the Terror of the mid-twentieth century. J. L. Talmon's famous book *The Origins of Totalitarian Democracy*, published in 1952, neatly encapsulated this connection between the two Terrors and expressly pointed to Rousseau as their originator, but the same thing had already been said by Carl Friedrich (without the language of "totalitarianism") soon after Hitler rose to power:

> the German situation . . . rather closely approached the radical democracy which Rousseau had envisaged, with very extreme powers vested in a popular majority (nor was this surprising, since the makers of the Weimar Constitution were filled with Rousseauistic ideas). The full significance of this set-up was hidden for a while by the multiple-party system. But the latent despotic powers of a popular majority were bound to appear as soon as such a majority could be built up.[25]

The democratic character of these despotic regimes was further popularized by Hannah Arendt in *The Origins of Totalitarianism* (1951), with such remarks as

> Hitler's rise to power was legal in terms of majority rule and neither he nor Stalin could have maintained the leadership of large populations, survived many interior and exterior crises, and braved the numerous dangers of relentless intra-party struggles if they had not had the confidence of the masses. (p. 306)[26]

And the idea became a staple of liberal political writing during the second half of the twentieth century.[27]

This trope rarely received the critical scrutiny it deserved. What is so striking in retrospect about all these works from the 1950s was their resolute refusal to link the totalitarian regimes of the interwar years specifically to the obvious and distinctive peculiarities of the period, and in particular to the catastrophe inflicted on the relevant societies by the First World War, followed by the communist revolutions in Russia, Germany, and Hungary (those in Germany and Hungary were suppressed by illegitimate armed force, which came close to suppressing the first as well). These facts so patently loomed over the politics of the interwar period that any serious attempt to explain why these societies lapsed into totalitarianism would surely have had to start with them, rather than with the inherent dangers of modern democracy.[28] The parallel with the Terror of 1793/94 holds even in this respect, since (as Engels, among others, observed) the Terror was obviously connected to the fact that the French state was facing an existential struggle for its existence in a war with the anti-revolutionary powers of Europe, and very little could be concluded from it about the dangers of even radical democracy in a nation at peace with its neighbors.[29]

Writers like Friedrich and Kennan also insisted, in the face of the evidence, that these regimes had come to power legitimately, in order to make the point that they were perversions of democracy.[30] But Hitler, for example, was granted dictatorial power not by a popular vote but by the Enabling Act passed by the Reichstag on 23 March 1933. The act passed because the Communist deputies who had been elected on 5 March 1933 were arrested under the Reichstag Fire Decree and could not take their seats, so that the meeting was inquorate; because the SPD members were intimidated by Nazi storm troopers in and around the chamber; and because of a number of other undemocratic procedures. Once in power, the Nazis proceeded to deprive Jews and other citizens of the vote, so that they never again had to face an election with universal suffrage.[31] Friedrich did at one point acknowledge this, remarking

> The events of the 21st of March, 1933 [the opening of the new Reichstag session without the Communists], were nothing more nor less than a repetition of Pride's Purge, of December 6th, 1648. When the detained Presbyterian M.P.'s demanded of the officers: "By what Law, by what Law?" Hugh Peters, Cromwell's secretary, had to admit: "It is by the Law of Necessity; truly, by the Power of the Sword."

So in what sense was this the consequence of "parliamentary absolutism"? What institutional structure can prevent a coup of this kind? Suppose that storm troopers surrounded the seat of a constitutional court, prevented some of the judges from attending and secured a ruling justifying dictatorship: how would that be different from the way the SA behaved in the Reichstag?[32] At the point at which "Necessity" enters, "Law" leaves, and the English revolutionaries were honest enough to admit it.[33] But the very fact that the Nazis had to mount an illegal coup of this kind is in itself evidence that the Weimar democratic institutions did not in fact permit the transition to dictatorship.

The same thing can be said about these writers' hostility not just to "parliamentary absolutism" but to the other democratic mechanism put in place by the authors of the Weimar constitution, the plebiscite. It is widely believed today that plebiscites are rather sinister, and that they have in the past characteristically been used to legitimate dictatorial or dangerous policies; the idea that representative assemblies offer the possibility of reasoned and well-informed discussion while plebiscites are governed by popular enthusiasm is still remarkably widespread. And yet, if one looks at the actual history of plebiscites, as I showed in *The Sleeping Sovereign*, it is far from clear that their track record was worse than that of representative assemblies. Virtually all European Social Democrat parties before World War I (which included the Communists) were committed to using the plebiscite,[34] as were the Progressives in the United States, and their experiences with them were not particularly destructive; if one simply takes the Weimar Republic, for example, the radicals of both Left and Right failed to win a single plebiscite of any significance. Only after the Enabling Act transformed the German constitution, and a large section of the population had begun to be disenfranchised, did Hitler begin to win plebiscites.

Why did the writers on totalitarianism ignore the extremely specific circumstances that had engendered the dictatorial regimes, circumstances that were unlikely to be repeated and indeed had not been experienced in the same way in the principal democratic states of the United Kingdom, France, and the United States? Ironically, it may be that for many of the German refugees, such as Arendt and (in a way) Friedrich, the motivation was a desire not to treat Germany as exceptional but to see in its disaster something that could befall any state that was not either lucky or careful. In this respect they were, reasonably enough, pushing back against the vulgar beliefs that there was something deeply wrong with the German character, or with the whole history of Germany, or with German philosophy; but they were curiously unwilling to say that the circumstances of the German disaster might nevertheless have been peculiar to it, and that no European nation could probably have withstood the social and political crisis into which the Great War had plunged Germany. There is a faint resemblance in the desire not to see Germany as exceptional to the way in which after 1918, in response to the "war guilt" clause of the Versailles Treaty (Article 231), both the Right and the Left in Germany converged on a narrative of the war in which it was presented as the almost inevitable consequence of a kind of doomsday machine constructed by the prewar diplomacy of the nations of Europe, though with the Left adding the argument that it was imperialist capitalism that had led to the construction of the machine.[35]

At all events, this account of totalitarianism clearly had enormous influence in the second half of the century and bolstered the construction during that period of the familiar institutions of the modern liberal state. Although the analysis of Nazism was important to this process, the immediate objective of course was to guard against the spread of communism; it should not be forgotten that (for example) the Communist Party was the largest party in the French Assembly after the first postwar election (and the first with universal suffrage including women) in 1945 and again after the 1946 election, when they entered the government. Largely because of American pressure they were ejected from the government the following year and never served in it again. The beginning of the Cold War in these years, as Sam Moyn has documented,[36] was a key part of the background to the constitutional discourse of the 1940s and 1950s across the Western world.

The essence of those liberal institutions was that straightforward democratic action would be checked in various ways: by entrenched constitutions (the West German *Grundgesetz* could not even be amended), independent constitutional courts, and (increasingly) international agreements such as those creating the EEC/EU, which functioned in effect as a further set of constitutional constraints on the domestic politics of the member nations. In general these institutions rendered virtually impossible the kind of socialist policies that had been canvassed in many countries before the Second World War,

involving quite widespread expropriation of private property—
except, notably, in the postwar United Kingdom, which resisted these
developments until the 1970s.[37] What fitted the institutions best, as
has often been observed, were the liberal capitalist regimes of Western Europe and North America, so that the economies and the legal
orders of these countries came to be entwined and hard to change
except at the margin—as even Thatcher found out!

A key feature of these structures was that the old notion of sovereignty began to disappear, both in the external sense of a sovereign
state vis-à-vis other states, but also in the more important internal
sense of a site of sovereign power *within* a state. Sieyès (once again)
had been prophetic, remarking, "This word [sovereignty] only looms
so large in our imagination because the spirit of the French, full of
royal superstitions, felt under an obligation to endow it with all the
heritage of pomp and absolute power which made the usurped sov-
ereignties shine."[38] Like Sieyès, the late-twentieth-century states resisted the idea of a single point at which a majoritarian vote could be
comprehensively decisive: instead, decisions were to be made in a
complex distributed fashion that frustrated the collective agency of
the citizens. But, as I wrote in my second chapter, structures of this
kind run the risk of engendering a vicious circle: popular resentment
at the lack of sovereignty scares the rulers of their countries and leads
them to insist even more on the necessity of entrenching safeguards
against majority rule. This is exactly what Rousseau described in the
letter to Mirabeau that I quoted earlier: "the conflict between men
and the laws, which makes for a perpetual intestine war in the State,
is the worst of all political States." The modern authoritarian populists whom Chambers cites, such as Erdoğan and Orbán, can be seen
as testimony to this: Orbán rages against the European Union, and
Erdoğan's followers directed much of their anger against the existing
Turkish constitution, itself a product of a military coup in 1982, but
amended as part of the the EU accession negotiations between 1999
and 2004 (though the history of military coups in modern Turkey
makes any conclusions about democratic institutions drawn from the
Turkish experience pretty nugatory).

If the first source of the apprehensions that people such as Chambers feel about radical democracy is the postwar liberal analysis of the

interwar years, the second source is a sense that parliamentarism in the modern world has failed. Ironically, this belief was also a central feature of the rise of the Right in the interwar years, with Fascism seen as a new representative system to replace the failed parliaments.[39] If elected parliaments no longer properly represent their populations, and if plebiscites are associated with populist despotism, it is not surprising that new forms of participation, such as sortition, are widely canvassed; sortition in particular appears to be a means of avoiding the corruption and distortion that electioneering engenders. It would be hard to deny that the spectacle of legislative assemblies in most modern states is a pretty depressing one; the dominance of party, in particular, as Rousseau perceived, renders impossible the old Sieyèsian ideal of responsible and well-informed discussion in a parliamentary setting. But what is striking about the turn to these new modes of representation is that, unlike the pre–First World War socialists who mostly also mistrusted the assemblies of their day, the people advocating them are also opposed to plebiscites. This is strange, given that the actual experience of plebiscites in our time, as well as in prewar Europe and America, is not in fact particularly discouraging (unless, of course, you happen to dislike the result). The quality of public debate over major issues such the Irish abortion and divorce referendums or the Brexit referendum, or even the annual ballot questions in Massachusetts, is far superior to the debates in their states' parliaments (not that, in the case of Brexit at least, that is saying very much). People sometimes point to the various plebiscites in American states that have on occasion banned gay marriage or entrenched low taxes, but those results are not peculiar to plebiscites: I do not think there is any measure passed by a referendum in an American state that did not have its counterpart in a measure passed by a legislature somewhere. We have no reason to think that there is any acceptable mechanism that will preclude such results in a democratic society, where constitutions are in the end open to popular amendment.

Even the turn against parties may not be justifiable. As I argue in the second chapter, parties are a necessary mechanism for coordinating the election of representatives and cannot—and should not—be wished away if we are going to have forms of representation at all; the history of fascism is testimony to the dangers in undermining the conventional party system in a democracy. They are necessary, to repeat what I said there, on an "active" view of voting, because they enable me to know that I am joining a large group who together may be able to effect some kind of change, where my vote has a good chance of being causally efficacious (sufficient, but not necessary). If voting is seen as purely representative—that is, if I simply wish my views to be made publically manifest in some fashion—then indeed parties are unnecessary and undesirable, and (in principle) everything could be decided by opinion polling! But if I want to feel that I am potentially able to change things, something like modern parties are probably necessary; I would add that the parties are under some obligation to the citizens to keep themselves effective, by forming as broad a coalition of voters as possible. Some proportional representation systems, on this view, run the danger of breaking up these pre-election coalitions, where the voters know with whom they are joining forces, and replacing them with post-election negotiations between politicians; though there are some proportional representation systems, including the French two-round method, of which this is not true.

In 1910 a royal commission was set up under the chairmanship of Lord Richard Cavendish to consider proposals for proportional representation in British Parliamentary elections. In the conclusion of its report, the commission observed the following.

> On the question whether the representation of all parties in proportion to their voting strength is in itself desirable, we may point out that it is not a fair argument against the present system that it fails to produce such a result, because it does not profess to do so. A general election is in fact considered by a large portion of the electorate of this country as practically a referendum on the question which of two Governments shall be returned to power. The view may be right or wrong, but it has to be taken account of in any discussion which turns on the composition of the House of Commons.[40]

This was a profound observation about British politics. The general public in Britain still sees an election as a kind of referendum, and

appeals by smaller parties to—in effect—leave the business of deciding who the government should be to the elected representatives have
always fallen on deaf ears. The decisive vote in the 2011 referendum
(appropriately enough) against an alternative vote system for Parliamentary elections was testimony to this intuitive sense on the part of
the electorate. And the great merit of this is that—just as in a properly
organized plebiscite—individual citizens know that they play an active role in making the decision about who should govern them.

But this does not really solve the central dilemma in modern politics, a dilemma that was (prophetically) at the heart of Rousseau's
theory. This is the poor fit between plebiscites (whether referendums
on single issues or a referendum on a government as a whole) and
representative institutions. Supporters of sortition, and of the various
other ways of changing the nature of representation, cannot avoid
this dilemma, except by reducing the significance of the collective
democratic vote. What they do in effect (and this was the point of my
contrast between Sieyès and Rousseau) is to return to a world in
which there are many different sites of representation, some "active"
(voting) and some "passive" (other forms of representation reminis-
cent of the premodern idea of the "virtual representation" enjoyed, if
that is not an inapproporiate word, by married women and other
disfranchised groups). This was precisely the world which the
democrats of the nineteenth and early twentieth centuries wished to
overturn, and to create instead a single site at which a collective
democratic decision could be made.

The institutions that they created managed to function effectively
until the second half of the twentieth century, as I wrote at the end of
my first chapter, because of a basic humility on the part of the representatives towards their electorates, a humility brought about both
by the nature of modern industrial production and by the exigencies
of the great wars. But these institutions are now failing; the sorry
post-Brexit events in the British Parliament are an example of this,
but the same thing is found across the world. In the United States, for
instance, where most states use plebiscites to change their constitutions or vote on ballot questions, there have been repeated cases of
state legislatures, both Republican and Democrat, finding ways to
delay or abort the implementation of clear-cut decisions by the

voters, most often on methods of redistricting or other ways of elimi-
nating the most obvious forms of corruption.[41] And the situation, as
we all know, is no better at the federal level.

The return of the old humility is made all the harder by the decrease in social mobility across much of the Western world. As John
Goldthorpe in particular has emphasized, significant numbers of
people moved from the working class into the "salariat," in what has
been called the "golden age of social mobility" in the middle decades
of the twentieth century. This was largely the result of structural
changes in class patterns, with the creation of new kinds of white-
collar jobs and the decline of old working-class occupations. But it
was a one-off event and has largely come to an end; men (especially)
are now more likely to be downwardly mobile than upwardly mobile.[42] This has had insidious psychological effects. Middle-class
people in the mid-twentieth century were quite likely to have had
working-class parents or siblings, and they would not find them cul-
turally alien (despite the novels of social dislocation which became
fashionable in 1950s Britain such as John Braine's *Room at the Top*).
This is no longer true to anything like the same degree, and something
more like the pre–Gilded Age class barriers have been recreated, with
obvious consequences for democratic politics.

One of the striking aspects of this is the trend detected by Roberto
Foa and Yascha Mounk, that in all the long-standing Western democracies there is a very precise correlation between the age of respondents in opinion polls and the degree of their commitment to
democracy. About 75 percent of those born in the 1930s believe that
it is "essential" to live in a democracy, but this falls steadily to little more
than 25 percent of those born in the 1980s. And lest this be thought
to be a relatively trivial question, the same is true of the answer
which people give to the question of whether a military takeover
would be legitimate: again, the older respondents are strongly opposed, and the younger ones far less so![43] The response of some
other political scientists to Mounk and Foa's findings was to say that
democratic values are still flourishing, as "tolerance of minorities"
has been steadily increasing over the same period.[44] But this goes to
the heart of what I have been arguing in this volume: for many
people today, particularly those born since the heyday of mass

democracy, the traditional apparatus of majoritarian voting is of increasing irrelevance.

What would it take to bring about the old humility and reinvigorate genuinely democratic politics? Rousseau himself was troubled by the question of how a population can come to think of themselves as active citizens, and his writings are full of attempts to answer this question, including such things as the civic festivals and games advocated in his *Considerations* on Poland; though it should not be forgotten that the bulk of the *Considerations* is devoted to suggestions for political and economic transformation, which he appears to have thought greatly outweighed in importance the cultural changes. In our time the problem is rather different, since we have electorates who have been accustomed for a century or more to full democratic activity. The impediment for those electorates in seeing themselves as active is not really psychological or cultural: it is principally the fact that there are in reality strong institutional barriers to the implementation of their wishes, barriers that at times of crisis become particularly visible and can intensify the crisis. Moreover the mass of the electorate do not have easy outlets for political activity other than the vote, particularly as participation in organizations such as unions dwindles. This is in marked contrast to the well-educated and eloquent sectors of the population, who feel (correctly) that they have plenty of ways of bringing influence to bear on the politics of their country, and who would be dismayed to find themselves reduced to the impotence of their fellow citizens. The idea of removing barriers to the full expression of what we might still call a "general will" appalls them, partly for the reasons I have discussed above (the sheer fear of majoritarianism) and partly because to them these barriers do not *feel* like impediments, and why should they feel that way to anyone else?

I doubt that the old humility can be engendered once more: the social and economic conditions of the modern world preclude it, though the turn away from a fully global economy after the pandemic might change that. Appeals to expand or protect democracy will fall on deaf ears unless the power of the vote is fully unleashed, and that is not very likely to happen spontaneously; indeed, the very people who express anxiety about the future of democracy are often the people keenest to find alternatives to voting. Instead, democracy of this old-fashioned kind now rests on a rather grimmer foundation: a mass electorate cannot be denied its power indefinitely without something like civil war being the result. It will turn in alarming ways against the institutions and the people it believes the source of its restraints, and attempts in the face of this to restrain it even more will create a vicious circle. It is hard for rulers to think of themselves as ruled, but this may in the long run be the only way that peace can be maintained in our societies.

NOTES

Introduction

1. Rousseau, *Political Writings*, 192–93, quoted in chapter 1 section III.

2. Cohen, *Rousseau: A Free Community of Equals* (Oxford: Oxford University Press, 2010).

Chapter 1

1. *Préliminaire de la Constitution. Reconnoissance et Exposition Raisonnée des Droits de l'Homme et du Citoyen. Lu les 20 et 21 Juillet 1789, au Comité de Constitution* (Paris: Chez Baudouin, 1789), 25–27, my translation.

2. *Sur la chose publique*, Sieyès's own term for the *respublica* (*Sieyès: Political Writings*, ed. Michael Sonenscher [Indianapolis, IN: Hackett Publishing, 2003], xxi). Sonenscher elsewhere translates it "public functions" (ibid., xxviii and 48).

3. *Préliminaire de la Constitution*, 20–22, my translation.

4. The Constitution of 1791 did not expressly limit the vote to men, giving it to "Ceux qui sont nés en France," etc., and women did in fact vote in the plebiscite on the Jacobin Constitution of the Year I (1793) (Serge Aberdam, "Deux occasions de participation féminine en 1793: Le vote sur la constitution et le partage des biens communaux," *Annales Historiques de la Révolution Française* 339 [2005], 17–34). It was the Constitution of the Year I, in a famous historical irony, that restricted it for the first time to "hommes" understood as males. See below for the history of female suffrage in France. The terms "active" and "passive" disappeared from public documents with the coming of universal male suffrage after the Revolution of 10 August 1792, and did not reappear with the repeal of universal suffrage in 1795, but even when universal male suffrage was reinstated, as it was under Napoleon and, finally, in 1848, the *category* of passive citizen persisted, since both women and foreigners continued to be "inactive"—in France, in the case of women, down to 1945; and in the case of foreigners, down to the present day. Sieyès himself continued to use the terminology: in his proposals for the Constitution of the Year VIII after the

Eighteenth Brumaire in 1799, he said that "the political association consists only of the *active* citizens, those who are engaged in the common project" (*Emmanuel Joseph Sieyès: The Essential Political Writings* ed. Oliver W. Lembcke and Florian Weber [Leiden: Brill, 2014], 194).

    5. See, e.g., his remarks in the *Metaphysics of Morals*, that

> this inequality is, however, in no way opposed to their freedom and equality as men, who together make up a people; on the contrary, it is only in conformity with the conditions of freedom and equality that this people can become a state and enter into a civil constitution. But not all persons qualify with equal right to vote within this constitution, that is, to be citizens and not mere associates in the state. For from their capacity to demand that all others treat them in accordance with the laws of natural freedom and equality as passive parts of the state it does not follow that they also have the right to manage the state itself as active members of it, the right to organize it or to cooperate for introducing certain laws. (Kant, *The Metaphysics of Morals*, trans. Mary Gregor [Cambridge: Cambridge University Press, 1991], 126)

The examples of passive citizens he gave there included "the blacksmith in India, who goes into people's houses to work on iron with his hammer, anvil, and bellows, as compared with the European carpenter or blacksmith who can put the products of his work up as goods for sale to the public" and who would therefore count as *active* (like, it should be said, Kant's father, a harness maker and citizen of Konigsberg). He did acknowledge, though, that "the concept of a passive citizen seems to contradict the concept of a citizen as such." For Kant's (rather complicated) intellectual relationship with Sieyès, see, e.g., François Azouvi and Dominique Bourel, *De Konigsberg à Paris: La Réception de Kant en France (1788–1804)* (Paris: Vrin, 1991), 77ff.

    6. "Contextualizing Hegel's Phenomenology of the French Revolution and the Terror," *Political Theory* 26 (1998): 39.

    7. Later in his life, Sieyès proposed a constitution that could not be amended at all. See my *The Sleeping Sovereign* (Cambridge: Cambridge University Press, 2016), 178–79.

    8. *Rights, Representation, and Reform* ed. Philip Schofield, Catherine Pease-Watkin, and Cyprian Blamires (Oxford: Oxford University Press, 2002), 272.

    9. *Dire . . . sur la question du Veto Royal* [September 1789], 17–18, my translation.

    10. *Observations sur le Rapport du Comité de Constitution, concernant la nouvelle Organisation de la France* [October 1789], 34–35, my translation.

    11. *Sieyès: Political Writings*, 98, 142.

    12. Ibid., 142.

    13. *Dire . . . sur la question du Veto Royal*, 14–15, my translation.

14. See on this question Nadia Urbinati, *Representative Democracy: Principles and Genealogy* (Chicago: University of Chicago Press, 2006), 151. In general, Urbinati's book is the best discussion of the Sieyèsian distinction.

15. "The representative system is nothing but an organisation by means of which a nation charges a few individuals to do what it cannot or does not wish to do herself. Poor men look after their own business; rich men hire stewards." Benjamin Constant, *Political Writings*, ed. Biancamaria Fontana (Cambridge: Cambridge University Press, 1988), 325–26.

16. In his essay on the English Reform Bill, Hegel praised Sieyès for having devised the constitutional structure of post-Jacobin France, the constitution that Hegel treated in his *Philosophy of Right* as the paradigm of a modern state (*Hegel's Political Writings*, trans. T. M. Knox, ed. Z. A. Pelczynski [Oxford: Oxford University Press, 1964], 322), while Marx observed in *The Holy Family* IV.4 that Proudhon "for the first time makes a real science of political economy possible. Proudhon's treatise *Qu'est-ce que la propriété?* is as important for modern political economy as Sieyès's work *Qu'est-ce que le tiers état?* for modern politics" (*Collected Works of Marx and Engels*, vol. IV [London: Lawrence and Wishart 1975], 32).

17. *The Holy Family* VI.3c, *Collected Works of Marx and Engels*, vol. IV, 122. He went on to give a fascinating interpretation of Napoleon.

> It was not the revolutionary movement as a whole that became the prey of Napoleon on 18 Brumaire . . . ; it was the liberal bourgeoisie. One only needs to read the speeches of the legislators of the time to be convinced of this. One has the impression of coming from the National Convention into a modern Chamber of Deputies.
>
> Napoleon represented the last battle of revolutionary terror against the bourgeois society which had been proclaimed by this same Revolution, and against its policy. Napoleon, of course, already discerned the essence of the modern state; he understood that it is based on the unhampered development of bourgeois society, on the free movement of private interest, etc. He decided to recognise and protect this basis. He was no terrorist with his head in the clouds. Yet at the same time he still regarded the state as an end in itself and civil life only as a treasurer and his subordinate which must have no will of its own. He perfected the Terror by substituting permanent war for permanent revolution.

Napoleon then fell for the same reason as the Jacobins, defeated by bourgeois society: "French businessmen took steps to anticipate the event that first shook Napoleon's power. Paris exchange-brokers forced him by means of an artificially created famine to delay the opening of the Russian campaign by nearly two months and thus to launch it too late in the year" (122–23). He would have gotten this idea from reading Philippe de Ségur's *Histoire de Napoléon et de la grande-armée pendant l'année 1812* (Paris, 1825), where Ségur says that

> Cependant une famine s'annonçait en France. Bientôt la crainte universelle accrut le mal par les précautions qu'elle suggéra. L'avarice, toujour prête à saisir toutes les voies de fortune, s'empara des grains, encore à vil prix, et attendit que la faim les lui redemendât au poids de l'or. Alors l'alarme devint générale. Napoléon fut forcé de suspendre son départ: impatient il pressait son conseil; mais les mesures à prendre étaient graves, sa présence nécessaire; et cette guerre où chaque heure perdue était irréparable, fut retardée de deux mois. (vol. I, 73)

The ambiguity Marx diagnosed in Napoleon is one that can be seen repeatedly in these kinds of European rulers; it was true, for example, of the interwar dictators, who combined a rhetoric of anti-capitalism with support for large private capitalistic enterprises. One might also say that, to some extent, this Napoleonic ambiguity remains true of the French state down to the present day.

18. Franz Mehring, *Karl Marx: The Story of his Life* (London: Allen and Unwin, 1936), 51.

19. For a sympathetic account of the much-discussed question of the intellectual relationship between Marx and Rousseau, see David Leopold, *The Young Marx* (Cambridge: Cambridge University Press, 2007), 262–71.

20. SC III.15. All quotations from *The Social Contract* are from the G.D.H. Cole translation, which to me is still Rousseau speaking in English. It was first published as an Everyman edition in 1913 (London: J. M. Dent), reprinted with amendments and additions by J. H. Brumfitt and J. C. Hall in 1973 (London: J. M. Dent), and again with a new introduction by Alan Ryan in 1993 (New York: A. A. Knopf). Citations are to the 1973 ed.

21. For example, Sonenscher in his introduction to *Sieyès: Political Writings*, xlvi–xlvii.

22. I mean by this the *Considerations on Poland*, the sketch for Corsica, and, in particular, the *Letters Written from the Mountain* together with the draft *History of Geneva*.

23. Guillaume François Berthier, *Observations sur Le Contrat Social de J.J. Rousseau* (Paris: Chez Mérigot le jeune, 1789), 66–71. This was published posthumously; Berthier had died in 1782. The *Avertissement de l'editeur* (v–vii) says that the work was begun as soon as the *Social Contract* appeared.

24. See "Nous allons voir des Etats-Généraux. . . ." Jean-Baptiste Salaville, *De l'organisation d'un état monarchique, ou Considérations sur les vices de la monarchie françoise, & sur la nécessité de lui donner une constitution* ([Paris] 1789), 74. While the Estates-General did not meet until May 1789, it was clear from the autumn of 1788 that they were to be summoned, and there was extensive argument over the rights of the Third Estate in late 1788. The chronology of *Considerations*, and its relationship

to *What Is the Third Estate* (which was published in January 1789), is unclear. Despite what Kenneth Margerison says (*Pamphlets & Public Opinion: The Campaign for a Union of Orders in the Early French Revolution* [West Lafayette, IN: Purdue University Press, 1998], 100–101), it is not obvious that Salaville had read Sieyès, and it is quite likely that the two works were written independently of each other, both during the controversy of 1788. One intriguing possibility is that it was the overt Rousseauism of *Considerations* that then provoked Sieyès in his works later in 1789 to deny the possibility of mandation, which was not an issue in *What Is the Third Estate*. The anonymous editor (allegedly Jean-Joseph Rive) of a third edition of the *Considerations* in 1789 (itself suggestive of an early date for the first edition) described Salaville's discussion of representation as "tout-à-fait neuve" (69).

25. Salaville, *De l'organisation d'un état monarchique*, 53–54. See Roger Barny, *Le triomphe du droit naturel: La constitution de la doctine révolutionnaire des droits de l'homme (1787–1789)*, *Annales Litteraires de l'Université de Besançon* 622 (1997), 124–26. Jean-Paul Rabaut Saint Etienne provided a rather different explanation of the role of the majority in establishing the general will: each voter recognizes that the general will expresses the common interest, but he votes in accordance with his own *amour de soi*. The plurality of votes expresses the "preponderant" interest, and in the absence of "privilege" the preponderant interest is the general will. *Question de droit public: Doit-on recueillir les voix, dans les états-généraux, par ordres, ou par têtes de délibérans?* ("En Languedoc," 1789), 9–16. For further examples of the use of Rousseau in the debates of 1789, see my *Sleeping Sovereign*, 143–56.

26. "What is a Representative? It is a Man to whom the Represented say: 'We cannot ourselves come to the National Assembly; but we charge you to carry our votes which are to be counted with yours'; and so whether they express their will by instructions which they give him, or by the trust which they put in their Representative, they decide on what he is going to vote for [*ils adoptent d'avance le voeu qu'il formera lui-même*]; their wills are made one [*identifiées*], but not their votes: they ought always to be counted in the sum total of votes from which comes the national will [*voeu national*]. . . . [T]he Representative of a larger number of Represented brings to the Assembly a larger number of effective votes [*voix effectives*]; &, since all the votes have the same degree of value, he ought necessarily to outweigh a Representative who only has the votes of a smaller number of Represented." *Sleeping Sovereign*, 76–78.

27. Though it was not printed until 1791, the dedication to the National Assembly is dated 30 October 1790 (p. xii), and it was accepted by the Assembly on 16 December (p. [299]). See my "From Rousseau to Kant" in *Markets, Morals and Politics: Jealousy of Trade and the History of Political Thought*, ed. Béla Kapossy, Isaac Nakhimovsky, Sophus Reinert, and Richard Whatmore (Cambridge, MA: Harvard University Press, 2018), 82–110.

28. *Supplément au Contract [sic] Social* (Paris, 1791), 20–21.

29. Rousseau, *Political Writings*, trans. and ed. F. M. Watkins (Edinburgh: Nelson, 1953), 185.

30. See, e.g., his remark that "the institution of serfdom in Poland makes it impossible . . . for the peasants to be armed immediately; arms in servile hands will always be more dangerous than useful to the state" (Rousseau, *Political Writings*, 239).

31. For an account of this fascinating encounter, see Thomas Bentley, *Journal of a Visit to Paris, 1776*, ed. Peter France (Falmer, UK: University of Sussex Library, 1977), 59–60. Some further details are recorded (at second hand) by David Williams in his *Incidents in My Own Life Which Have Been Thought of Some Importance*, ed. Peter France (Falmer, UK: University of Sussex Library, 1980), 20–22.

32. E.g., Wilmoore Kendall in his edition of *The Government of Poland* (Indianapolis, IN: Hackett, 1985), xiv.

33. *Political Writings*, 192–93.

34. *Collected Writings of Rousseau*, vol. IX, ed. Christopher Kelly and Eve Grace, trans. Christopher Kelly and Judith R. Bush (Hanover, NH: Dartmouth College, 2001), 293.

35. *The Civil War in France*, address 3, *Collected Works of Marx and Engels*, vol. XXII (London: Lawrence and Wishart, 1975), 332. And see the *Manifeste du Comité des Vingt Arrondissements* (March 1871) in *Affiches, Professions de Foi, Documents Officiels, Clubs & Comités pendant la Commune*, ed. Firmin Maillard (Paris: E. Dentu, 1871), 114, calling for "La souveraineté du suffrage universel, restant toujours maître de lui-même et pouvant se convoquer et se manifester incessament; Le principe de l'élection appliqué a tous les fonctionnaires ou magistrats; La responsabilité des mandataires, et par conséquent leur révocabilité permanente; Le mandat impératif, c'est-à-dire précisant et limitant le pouvoir et la mission du mandataire."

36. In 1620, the City of York appointed a fifteen-man committee to draw up the instructions, and similar practices are documented in Berwick, Great Yarmouth, Southwark, and many other boroughs—above all, London. Even in county elections, with much larger electorates and no institutional structures like a town council to manage the drafting of instructions, the voters could agree to issue specific commands to their members: in Cheshire in 1624, the presiding officer, the sheriff, after urging the voters to choose two able candidates, also urged them to "go a little further and . . . command your knights that if there be occasion offered they shall in the name of their country, and as by special command of the country, make public protestation against a toleration of religion or the repealing of laws formerly made against recusants." This suggests that "going a little further" than simply electing a representative was a perfectly familiar feature of seventeenth-century elections, and it certainly continued into the eighteenth century. See *The History of Parliament: the House of Commons 1604–1629*, vol. I, ed. Andrew Thrush and John P. Ferris

(Cambridge: Cambridge University Press, 2010), 456; and the article on Bristol in *The History of Parliament: The House of Commons, 1754–1790*, vol. I, ed. L. Namier and J. Brooke (London: Secker and Warburg, 1964).

37. While Bentham was rather hostile to mandation, he was an enthusiast for the recall of deputies when their electors believed that they had not represented their wishes properly. See *Constitutional Code*, chap. 4, art. 2, in *Constitutional Code*, vol. I, ed. F. Rosen and J. H. Burns (Oxford: Oxford University Press, 1983), 26. It should also be noted that in addition to this, he advocated annual elections.

38. "On the 'Misogyny' of Jean-Jacques Rousseau: *The Letter to d'Alembert* in Historical Context," *French Historical Studies* 25 (2002): 91–114. The other "misogynist" text is of course *Emile*, but there too the issue is complex: much of the denunciation of women is a denunciation of the way that, like men, they have been corrupted by modern society, and there is one passage where he applauds their role in politics: "Every great revolution began with the women. Through a woman Rome gained her liberty, through a woman the plebeians won the consulate, through a woman the tyranny of the decemvirs was overthrown; it was the women who saved Rome when besieged by Coriolanus." *Emile, or Education*, trans. Barbara Foxley (London: J. M. Dent, 1921), 354.

39. Cole translation emended by me. Last sentence is a footnote.

40. His unfinished *History of the Government of Geneva* seems to belong broadly with his *Letters Written from the Mountain*, though it was not published until 1861.

41. "[T]hat primitive Contract, that essence of Sovereignty, that empire of the Laws, that institution of Government, that manner of confining it in various degrees in order to balance authority with force, that tendency to usurpation, those periodic assemblies, that skill in getting rid of them, finally that imminent destruction that menaces you and that I wished to prevent; isn't this stroke for stroke the image of your Republic, since its birth up to this day?" Sixth Letter from the Mountain in *Collected Writings of Rousseau*, vol. IX, 233.

42. Ibid., 113–14. Kelly and Bush translate "aussi démocratique qu'il était possible" as "as democratic as possible," but this is subtly different from the French.

43. Letter to Etienne Dumont, 14 May 1802, in *The Correspondence of Jeremy Bentham*, vol. VII, ed. J. R. Dinwiddy (Oxford: Oxford University Press, 1988), 26.

44. *Plan of Parliamentary Reform* (London: R. Hunter, 1817), 9. He appears to have thought something similar in his earlier "*Projet* of a Constitutional Code for France": "By a French citizen is to be understood 1. all such as have had their birth on French ground: 2. all such as shall have thought proper to inscribe their names in the register of any parish in France, renouncing at the same time their allegiance to every other state." *The Collected Works of Jeremy Bentham: Rights, Representation, and Reform: Nonsense upon Stilts and Other Writings on the French Revolution*, ed. Philip Schofield, Catherine Pease-Watkin, and Cyprian Blamires (Oxford: Oxford

University Press, 2002), 231. "Every man ought at all times to be free, upon proper notice, to chuse what state he will belong to. It is much more material to individuals to enjoy this right uncontrouled, than it can be to the community to controul it" (249–50). Any foreigner could simply put their name on the electoral roll whenever they chose.

45. *The Civil War in France*, address 3, *Collected Works of Marx and Engels*, vol. XXII, 338. The Commission for Elections on 26 March 1871 pronounced as follows in answer to the question, "*Les étrangers peuvent-ils être admis à la Commune?*"

Considérant que le drapeau de la Commune est celui de la République universelle

Considérant que toute cité a le droit de donner le titre de citoyen aux étrangers qui la servent;

Que cet usage existe depuis longtemps chez des nations voisines

Considérant que le titre de membre de la Commune étant une marque de confiance plus grande encore que le titre de citoyen, comporte implicitement cette dernière qualité,

La commission est d'avis que les étrangers peuvent être admis et vous propose l'admission du citoyen Frankel.

Firmin Maillard, ed., *Affiches, Professions de Foi, Documents Officiels, Clubs & Comités pendant la Commune* (Paris: E. Dentu, 1871), 146.

46. *Recueil de documents relatifs à la convocation des États généraux de 1789*, vol. I, ed. Armand Brette (Paris: Imprimerie Nationale, 1894), 77.

47. François Furet, "The Monarchy and the Procedures for the Elections of 1789," *Journal of Modern History* 60 (1988): Supplement, *Rethinking French Politics in 1788* 67.

48. See the detailed study by René Larivière, "Les femmes dans les assemblées de paroisses pour les élection aux Etats Généraux de 1789," *Bulletin d'Histoire Economique et Sociale de la Révolution Française* (1974): 123–56; figures for Périgord are on p. 138, including the observation that the voters were "veuves le plus souvent, mais aussi femmes mariées avec ou representant leur époux, mères avec leur fils ou célibataires." In the small Norman village of Crulai in 1708, 66 out of 310 *chefs de famille* were widows and on the tax rolls. Jacques Dupâquier, "Des roles de tailles a la démographie historique: L'exemple de Crulai" *Population* 24 (1969): 98.

49. Furet, "The Monarchy and the Procedures," 64–65. The electorate for earlier meetings of the Estates-General was studied by J. Russell Major in *The Deputies to the Estates General in Renaissance France* (University of Wisconsin Press 1960). He concluded that, as in 1789, there was a great deal of local variation, but by the sixteenth century the suffrage was often very extensive (125–27); he did not investigate the question of women voting.

50. Serge Aberdam, "Deux occasions de participation féminine en 1793: le vote sur la constitution et le partage des biens communaux," *Annales Historiques de la Révolution*

Française 339 (2005) : 17–34. As both he and Larivière observe, women were expressly given the vote in 1793 in the assemblies that were charged with dividing up the old common lands, so they were not entirely excluded from political processes.

51. See Derek Hirst, *The Representative of the People? Voters and Voting in England under the Early Stuarts* (CUP 1975) pp 18–19.

52. Pierre Antonetti, *Histoire de la Corse* (Paris: Editions Laffont, 1973), 267.

53. Lynn Lubamersky, "Women and Political Patronage in the Politics of the Polish-Lithuanian Commonwealth," *Polish Review* 44 (1999): 269.

54. The first few pages of the first volume of the *Livre des Habitants* yield a number of widows' names, e.g., Ysabeau Monon, *relaissée* of Charles Quinal (p. 3), Janne *relaissée* "d'ung nommé Langloisse" (p. 10), and Pernette Marchant *relaissée* of Jehan Le Gras (p. 23). See *Livre des Habitants de Genève, Tome I, 1549–1560* ed. Paul-F. Geisendorf (Geneva: Librairie Droz, 1957).

55. *Collected Works of Jeremy Bentham*, ed. Schofield, Pease-Watkin, and Blamires, 246 ff. Although the editors date this to 1789, and regard it as a response to the "Articles of the Constitution" promulgated in October 1789, this dating is not absolutely convincing. The radical character of the proposals have more the tone of something produced in 1792, and it also seems to track the structure and contents of the actual constitution as issued in September 1791. It is tempting to associate the *Projet* with the invitation issued to *savants* across Europe in October 1792 to produce new constitutional proposals. As we know from a report on these proposals in April 1793 (Jean-Denis Lanjuinais, *Rapport lu le lundi 9 avril 1793, à la Convention nationale, au nom du Comité des six, établi pour analyser les projets de constitution: sur le titre II du projet du Comité des neuf, concernant l'état des citoyens & les conditions nécessaires pour en exercer les droits*) (Paris, 1793), many of them had proposed female suffrage, including David William's *Observations sur la dernière constitution de la France*, one of the few that were printed. Although the expressed intention in September 1792 was to abolish the monarchy, the Constitution of 1791 with a king was still in force, and the fact that Bentham's *Projet* includes a king is not conclusive evidence against a later date; William's *Incidents in My Own Life Which Have Been Thought of Some Importance* (ed. Peter France, [Brighton: University of Sussex Library, 1980], 28) records that his own invitation was "only to write down my objections to the Constitution of 1791." Nor is the fact that Bentham refers to a proposal in 1789 to have staggered elections to the Assembly proof that the *Projet* was drafted before the 1791 Constitution took its final shape, as the editors thought. It is also worth noting that the *Projet* deals in some detail with the divisions of territory, something the *savants* seem to have been asked to consider. See Lanjuinais, *Rapport fait a la Convention nationale au nom de son Comité des six, établi pour analyser les projets de constitution: sur le titre premier du projet du Comité des neuf, concernant la division du territoire de la République* (Paris, 1793).

56. Pierre Guyomar, *Le partisan de l'égalité politique entre les individus* (Paris, 1793), 14. See also his strongly majoritarian remarks to the Assembly in 1795, attacking the system of indirect election under the Directory (and incidentally drawing the kind of parallel between America and France that I discussed in *The Sleeping Sovereign*):

> C'est à la majorité, et non à la minorité, de faire les élections dans le vrai système représentatif. En effet, les représentants, nommés par les électeurs, ne sont pas les élus du peuple, mais les délégués des corps électoraux. Une fois que le peuple aurait nommé ses électeurs, il ne serait plus rien, tandis qu'il doit être dans le système représentatif, la source immédiate d'où doivent découler tous les pouvoirs. Forcé par l'étendue du territoire de déléguer le droit de faire des lois, il est contraire au système représentatif de confier à d'autres le droit d'élection. Bref, réduire le droit de cité à nommer des électeurs, c'est le réduire à fort peu de choses, c'est pour ainsi dire l'anéantir. En effet, la volonté ne se représente pas; aussi, à la majorité seule du peuple appartient le droit d'accepter ou de rejeter le pacte social. À la majorité du peuple aussi appartient le droit immédiat d'élection. Les Américains, fidèles au vrai principe du système représentatif, ont conservé le droit immédiat d'élection; ils sont nos frères aînés en Révolution, leur République est florissante.

Bernard Gainot, "Pierre Guyomar et la revendication démocratique dans les débats autour de la constitution de l'an III," in *1795, pour une République sans Révolution*, ed. Roger Dupuy (Rennes: Presses Universitaires de Rennes, 1996), 261–73.

57. "Rousseau a proclamé d'avance, sans l'appeler par son nom, le suffrage universel, et si l'Assemblée nationale avait été pénétrée de son esprit, elle n'aurait pas commis la faute irréparable de diviser la France nouvelle en citoyens actifs et en citoyens passifs." See Jean Jaurès, "Les idées politiques et sociales de Jean-Jacques Rousseau" (1889), ed. Gilles Candar and Stéphanie Roza, in *Cahiers Jaurès* 231–32 (2019): 189–92, quotation on p. 202. Jaurès also stressed the relevance of the sovereign/government distinction in Rousseau, and was even willing to see the United States as a kind of Rousseauian state for this reason, something of which I was unaware when I wrote *The Sleeping Sovereign*.

58. I am thinking of course of J. L. Talmon's *The Origins of Totalitarian Democracy* (London: Secker & Warburg, 1952), which (though concerned with both varieties of totalitarianism) linked Rousseau more to Soviet Communism than to Nazism.

59. E.g., Frederick Neuhouser, *Rousseau's Critique of Inequality* (Oxford: Oxford University Press, 2014). Other cases could include Istvan Hont's reading of Rousseau as a kind of Smithian: see Istvan Hont, *Politics in Commercial Society: Jean-Jacques Rousseau and Adam Smith*, ed. Béla Kapossy and Michael Sonenscher (Cambridge, MA: Harvard University Press, 2015).

60. Kenneth J. Arrow, *Social Choice and Individual Values*, 2nd ed. (New Haven, CT: Yale University Press, 1963), 85 and n. 24. See Brian Barry, *Political Argument*

(London: Routledge, 1965), 292–93; Bernard Grofman and Scott L. Feld, "Rousseau's General Will: A Condorcetian Perspective," *American Political Science Review* 82 (1988): 567–76; David M. Estlund, Jeremy Waldron, Bernard Grofman and Scott L. Feld, "Democratic Theory and the Public Interest: Condorcet and Rousseau Revisited," *American Political Science Review* 83 (1989): 1317–40. For the most thoughtful discussion of the argument, though one that is broadly in sympathy with it, see Joshua Cohen, *Rousseau: A Free Community of Equals* (Oxford: Oxford University Press, 2010), 78–82.

61. Bruno Bernardi, *La Fabrique des Concept: Recherches sur l'Invention Conceptuelle de Rousseau* (Paris: Champion, 2006), 421; Michael Sonenscher, *Sans-culottes: An Eighteenth-Century Emblem in the French Revolution* (Princeton, NJ: Princeton University Press, 2008), 117.

62. "Enim vero in moralibus hautquaquam absurdum eft, particulares illas voluntates, ex quarum conspiratione voluntas universitatis resultat, destitui aliqua facultate, qua huic inest. *Le droit de la nature et des gens, ou Système général des principes les plus importans de la morale, de la jurisprudence et de la politique*, trans. J. Barbeyrac (Amsterdam: G. Kuyper 1706)." Similarly, at VII.2.5 the Barbeyrac Pufendorf talks of the "resolutions" of the sovereign which "passent pour la volonté de tous en général & de chacun en particulier"; this is, I think, an unacknowledged quotation from du Verdus's translation of Hobbes's *De Cive* (1660) in *Les élémens de la politique de Monsieur Hobbes*, trans. François Du Verdus (Paris: Chez Henty Le Gras, 1660), which also talks about the will of the sovereign being taken for "la volonté de tous eux en general, & de chacun en particulier" (V.6), a translation of *omnes et singuli*, which Sorbiere in his more widely read translation of 1649 did not use.

63. "La volonté de tous est donc l'ordre, la règle suprême; & cette règle générale & personnifiée est ce que j'appelle le souverain." For one of the first of Rousseau's followers saying the same, see Guillaume-Joseph Saige, *Catéchisme du citoyen: ou, élements du droit public françois, par demandes et par réponses* (published and then immediately condemned in 1775): "by the essence of the civil state, sovereign authority can only legitimately reside in the body of the people, since the will of all [*volonté de tous*] is the only thing which invariably tends to the main purpose of a political institution." Keith Baker, "A classical republican in eighteenth-century Bordeaux: Guillaume-Joseph Saige," in his *Inventing the Revolution* (Cambridge: Cambridge University Press, 1990), 128–52; Roger Barny, *Prélude Idéologique à la Révolution Française: Le Rousseauisme avant 1789, Annales Litteraires de l'Université de Besançon* 315 (1985): 101–20. The *Letters* were published at the end of 1764 both as a defense of *The Social Contract* and as an intervention in Genevan politics; they have been remarkably neglected by writers on Rousseau's political ideas, with the conspicuous exception of Joshua Cohen.

64. "[L]a Loi, qui n'est que l'expression de la volonté générale, est bien le résultat de tous les intérêts particuliers combinés & balancés par leur multitude." Rousseau,

Oeuvres Complètes, vol. III, ed. Michel Launay (Paris: Editions du Seuil, 1971), 541; *Political Writings*, 199.

65. "When men have met to erect a commonwealth, they are, almost by the very fact that they have met, a *Democracy*. From the fact that they have gathered voluntarily, they are understood to be bound by the decisions made by agreement of the majority. And that is a *Democracy*, as long as the convention lasts, or is set to reconvene at certain times and places. For a convention whose will is the will of all the citizens has *sovereign power*. And because it is assumed that each man in this convention has the right to vote, it follows that it is a *Democracy*." *De Cive* VII.5, in Hobbes, *On the Citizen*, trans. Michael Silverthorne, ed. Richard Tuck (Cambridge: Cambridge University Press, 1998), 94.

66. *Political Writings*, 199.

67. *Collected Writings of Rousseau*, vol. IX, 306. I would like to thank Nathaniel Hiatt for helping me see the significance of this passage.

68. "A Paradox in the Theory of Democracy," in *Philosophy, Politics and Society*, ed. Peter Laslett and W. G. Runciman (Oxford: Basil Blackwell, 1962), 71–87.

69. "No Paradox in Democracy," *Political Studies* 18 (1970): 514–17.

70. This was Salaville's view also: he quoted just this passage on giving opinions, and explained it by saying that when I vote "I can be wrong and consequently vote against my will, which is aimed at the maintenance and prosperity of the association. It is just the same, whatever the number of votes allied to mine, if the majority is not on my side" (*De l'organisation d'un état monarchique*, 54).

71. "Quand on recherche comment l'idée d'un si terrible despotisme a pu venir dans la tête de gens qui ne prêchent que la liberté, on voit qu'elle tient à l'illusion très commune de confondre la liberté avec l'autorité & avec le gout trop naturel de la domination. . . . Elle tient aux idées de Mr. Rousseau, qui croyant avec *Hobbes* que les hommes sont nés ennemis les uns des autres, & croyant de plus que nous n'avons pas de pires ennemis que nos supérieures, y remédie comme lui par le Despotisme, mais en le plaçant differemment. Car au lieu que Hobbes donne le pouvoir arbitraire à un Prince, Mr. Rousseau qui ne connoit point les milieux, donne un semblable pouvoir à la multitude." [Jacob Vernet], *Lettre d'un citoyen de Genève à un autre citoyen. Le 15 Février 1768* (n.p., 1768), 72–73. Vernet also attacked the passage in *Letters Written from the Mountain* in which Rousseau pleaded, "Were it bad in itself, take it all together; by that alone it will become the best." He described the sentiment as "something urged in a spirit of hostility to attack and conquer [Rousseau's opponents in Geneva] at any cost, but which should never be adopted—and even less persevered in—by enlightened and peaceful Patriots" ("conseil donné dans un esprit d'hostilité pour attaquer & vaincre à tout prix, mais qui ne devoit jamais être adopté, & encore moins suivi obstinément, par des Patriotes éclairés & pacifiques"). Ibid., 62.

72. E.g., "it is not in men's power to deprive evidence of the absolute empire which it exercises on them by nature, nor to prevent its despotic power from being (through the means of its public recognition) the constant principle of a physical force to which all other forces are obliged to submit" ("il n'est pas au pouvoir des hommes de faire perdre à l'évidence l'empire absolu qu'elleexerce naturellement sur eux, et d'empêcher que par le moyen de sa publicité, son autorité despotique ne soit toujours le principe constant d'une force physique à laquelle toute autre force et obligeé de céder"). Pierre-Paul Le Mercier de La Rivière, *L'Ordre Naturel et Essentiel des Sociétés Politiques*, vol. I (London and Paris, 1767), 182–83. (See also the edition by Edgard Depitre [Paris: Paul Geuthner, 1910], p. 84.) The same year, Quesnay (described by Mirabeau to Rousseau in his reply to the letter of 26 July as "the Confucius of Europe") published his famous defense of the modern Chinese government as an enlightened despotism operating on physiocratic principles ("Despotism in China, a translation of François Quesnay's 'Le Despotisme de la Chine,' Paris, 1767," in Lewis A. Maverick, *China a Model for Europe*, vol. II [San Antonio, TX: P. Anderson, 1946]).

73. *Rousseau: The Social Contract and Other Later Political Writings*, ed. Victor Gourevitch (Cambridge: Cambridge University Press, 1997), 270.

74. On squaring the circle, see D'Alembert's article "Quadrature du cercle" in *Encyclopédie, ou dictionnaire raisonné des sciences, des arts et des métiers*, vol. XIII, eds. Denis Diderot and Jean le Rond d'Alembert (Neuchâtel: Chez Samuel Faulche, 1765), 639–41, where he described the attempt to do so as "pointless" (*inutile*) and called for work on a proper proof of its impossibility. On longitudes, see, e.g., Guy Boistel, "Pierre Bouguer, commissaire pour la marine et expert pour les longitudes: Un opposant au développement de l'horlogerie de marine au xviiie siècle?" *Revue d'histoire des sciences* 63 (2010): 121–59. It may be significant that Rousseau was the son of an expert clockmaker and may have been well aware of the difficulties involved in making a chronometer, which even John Harrison did not entirely overcome.

75. *Political Writings*, 161–62. We can compare this remark with Hobbes's observation in the *Elements of Law* II.10.8 that "seeing right reason is not existent, the reason of some man, or men, must supply the place thereof; and that man, or men, is he or they, that have the sovereign power." See *The Elements of Law Natural & Politic*, ed. Ferdinand Toennies (Cambridge: Cambridge University Press, 1928), 150.

76. "The Right of the People to Review Judge-Made Law," *Outlook*, 8 August 1914, 843ff.

77. See in particular Hobbes's remark in chapter 11 of *Leviathan*: "benefits oblige; and obligation is thraldome; and unrequitable obligation, perpetuall thraldome; which is to ones equall, hatefull" (ed. Richard Tuck [Cambridge: Cambridge University Press, 1996], 71). This drew on Seneca's essay "De Beneficiis," with its remarks such as "Repeated reference to our services wounds and crushes the spirit of the other.

He wants to cry out like the man who, after being saved from the proscription of the triumvirs by one of Caesar's friends, because he could not endure his benefactor's arrogance, cried 'Give me back to Caesar!'" (Loeb ed. II.11, in Seneca, *Moral Essays*, vol. III trans., John W. Basore, Loeb Classical Library [Cambridge, MA: Harvard University Press, 1935], 67).

Chapter 2

1. Though the *nomothetai*, who were deputed to consider proposed legislation, could be chosen by lot.

2. The pope is technically elected by the clergy of the city of Rome, though the clergy are now cardinals drawn from all round the world. Since 1179 there has usually (but not invariably) been a supermajority requirement. An interesting contrast can be drawn with the choice of the pope of the Coptic Church, where a boy draws one of three names out of a chalice—a survival of sortition in part of the old Hellenistic world. The geographical distribution of majority voting, or indeed voting of any kind, deserves further study. It seems not to have been used in ancient China; it does not figure in the Old Testament; and examples in ancient India that have been described as "election" turn out on inspection to be cases of sortition. Sortition seems to be close to universal in human societies, but majority voting is (on the global scale) an unusual phenomenon, testimony perhaps to its psychological difficulty.

3. In his *Discourse on Political Economy*, in *The Social Contract and the Discourses* trans. G.D.H. Cole, revised and augmented J.H. Brumfitt and John C. Hall (Everyman's Library) (London: J. M. Dent 1973), 122. The Roman comitia was not fully deliberative but a mechanism for permitting a very large body of citizens to vote after hearing a rather limited set of addresses from private citizens. See Andrew Lintott, *The Constitution of the Roman Republic* (Oxford: Oxford University Press, 1999), 45–46.

4. The first modern defenses of sortition (in their case, its use to choose a reformed US House of Representatives) may have been Ernest Callenbach and Michael Phillips, *A Citizen Legislature* (Bodega, CA: Banyan Tree, 1985). This was reprinted in 2008 by Imprint Academic (Exeter, UK) and bound with an English version of their proposal by Keith Sutherland, *A People's Parliament*. I have chosen to use Guerrero as the representative of this view, but Sutherland has done important work in this area. For Guerrero's views, see in particular his "Against Elections: The Lottocratic Alternative," *Philosophy and Public Affairs* 42 (2014): 135–78. Footnote 19 on p. 157 is a good survey of the modern literature on sortition, but it does not include Bernard Manin's important account of the history of the turn from sortition to election, *The Principles of Representative Government* (Cambridge: Cambridge University Press, 1997).

5. Eric Nelson, "Representation and the Fall," *Modern Intellectual History* 17(3) (2020), 647–76.

6. See Greg Conti, *Parliament the Mirror of the Nation* (Cambridge: Cambridge University Press, 2019). And Philip Pettit, "Representation, Responsive and Indicative," *Constellations* 17 (2010): 426–34.

7. Except in the sense that it might be evidence for some kind of distortion in the electoral process that an assembly consists entirely of one sort of person. But on the Rousseauian account, it is not conclusive evidence, nor is it intrinsically undesirable, as long as the mandates of the electors are obeyed by the delegates.

8. *Socialism: An Economic and Sociological Analysis*, trans. J. Kahane (Indianapolis, IN: Liberty Fund, 1981), 12.

9. See, e.g., Dave Denison, "Defeating the Voters," *Baffler*, 14 May 2019.

10. *Free Riding* (Cambridge, MA: Harvard University Press, 2008).

11. The Romans managed to combine a secret ballot with serial voting by (in effect) announcing a rolling count and withdrawing candidates when they secured a majority; this was also a practical way of avoiding Condorcet cycling in elections such as those for the tribunate where there were multiple candidates.

12. See Kenneth J. Arrow, "Gifts and Exchanges", in *Altruism, Morality, and Economic Theory* ed. Edmund S. Phelps (New York: Russell Sage Foundation, 1975), 17–18; and Thomas Nagel, "Comment," in ibid., 65. Arrow's paper was also published in *Philosophy and Public Affairs* 1 (1972): 343–62. Later discussions are by James Andreoni, "Giving with Impure Altruism: Applications to Charity and Ricardian Equivalence," *Journal of Political Economy* 97 (1989): 1447–58; Andreoni, "Impure Altruism and Donations to Public Goods: A Theory of Warm-Glow Giving," *Economic Journal* 100 (1990): 464–77; and Robert Goodin, *Reasons for Welfare* (Princeton, NJ: Princeton University Press, 1988), 155–57. Goodin coined the appealing term "agency altruism"—see, e.g., Nancy Flobre and Robert Goodin, "Revealing Altruism," *Review of Social Economy* 62 (2004): 1–25.

13. In this context, there is a persistent and revealing confusion in the literature on choice between "choice" and "preference." Preference does not imply action, so I can (for example) have preferences with regard to the past—I prefer the Girondins to the Jacobins. But I cannot *choose* the Girondins over the Jacobins (unless I am being asked to do something now, such as rank them in a quiz).

14. *Law and Disagreement* (Oxford: Oxford University Press, 1999), 113–14.

15. He rejected a simple coin toss as a means of making a decision, but a representative sample of citizens seems, as I say, to meet his criteria.

16. *Social Contract* IV.2. On supermajorities in general, see the appropriately critical remarks by Melissa Schwartzberg in *Counting the Many* (Cambridge: Cambridge University Press, 2013).

17. Notable exceptions are Nancy Rosenblum, *On the Side of the Angels: An Appreciation of Parties and Partisanship* (Princeton, NJ: Princeton University Press 2008); and Ian Shapiro and Frances Rosenbluth, *Responsible Parties* (New Haven, CT: Yale University Press, 2018).

18. The Social Contract *and Other Later Political Writings*, ed. Victor Gourevitch (Cambridge: Cambridge University Press, 1997), 270.

19. The first took the vote away from naturalized Jews (about a quarter of the German Jewish population), and the second from all Jews. It is also worth bearing in mind that Hitler rose to power not through a plebiscite (the Nazis lost the two plebiscites they supported under the Weimar constitution) but through an act passed by an assembly of representatives, the Enabling Act of March 1933, and that the one attempt to halt his rise through a case in a constitutional court, the *Staatsgerichthof*, failed when the judges (all appointed under the Weimar governments) ruled in the Nazis' favor. See David Dyzenhaus, "Legal Theory in the Collapse of Weimar: Contemporary Lessons?" *American Political Science Review* 91 (1997): 121–34. A less vicious but still pertinent example would be the way the Protestant ruling class of the North of Ireland in the 1970s used an archaic property franchise in the local government of the province to ensure a large Protestant majority, at a time when the rest of the United Kingdom had moved (in 1945) to universal suffrage in local government.

20. Daniela Cammack has drawn my attention to a remarkable passage by Demosthenes, which Rousseau (who admired Demosthenes) will have known. In it, Demosthenes attacked the Athenians for being "double-dealers" because "they praise the Spartans in all other respects, they do not imitate the most admirable of all their practices, but rather do the very opposite. For they say, men of Athens, that among them [the Spartans] each man airs any opinion he may have until the question is put, but when the decision has been ratified, they all approve it and work together, even those who opposed it. Therefore, though few, they prevail over many and by actions well timed they get what they cannot get by war." *Exordium* 35.2–3, in *Orations*, vol. VII, trans. Norman W. DeWitt and Norman J. DeWitt, Loeb Classical Library (Cambridge, MA: Harvard University Press, 1949), 149.

21. *Sur la necessité de faire ratifier le constitution par les citoyens*, in Condorcet, *Oeuvres IX* (Paris, 1847), 415, translated in *Condorcet: Foundations of Social Choice and Political Theory*, trans. and ed. Iain McLean and Fiona Hewitt (Aldershot: Edward Elgar, 1994), 272.

22. *The Papers of Thomas Jefferson*, vol. XV, ed. Julian P. Boyd (Princeton, NJ: Princeton University Press, 1958), 379–99.

23. Christian List and Philip Pettit, *Group Agency: The Possibility, Design and Status of Corporate Agents* (Oxford: Oxford University Press, 2011). It is worth bearing in mind that a characteristic of many of these early democrats (especially Bentham and Marx) was a fear of "fictions" or "reifications." I would say the same was true of Hobbes,

despite the frequent attribution to him of a notion of corporate identity; as in the case of his ideas on democracy, he was much more ambiguous than is often recognized.

24. Letter to Samuel Kercheval, *The Writings of Thomas Jefferson*, vol. XV, ed. Albert Ellery Bergh (Memorial Ed.) (Washington, DC: Jefferson Memorial Association, 1907), 42–43.

25. The United Kingdom has an electorate of 45 million and a death rate in the adult population of about 540,000 per annum, so half the current electorate will be dead after approximately 42.5 years.

26. The British government finally paid off the last of its National War Bonds, issued in 1917, in 2015. Shortly afterwards, it paid off some Consols, which contained debts incurred at the time of the South Sea Bubble, the Napoleonic Wars, etc.

27. In the debate in the Commons on 23 October 1943 about rebuilding the Chamber after it was bombed, Churchill urged that it should remain rectangular, to express its adversarial character, and then added

> The second characteristic of a Chamber formed on the lines of the House of Commons is that it should not be big enough to contain all its Members at once without over-crowding and that there should be no question of every Member having a separate seat reserved for him. The reason for this has long been a puzzle to uninstructed outsiders and has frequently excited the curiosity and even the criticism of new Members. Yet it is not so difficult to understand if you look at it from a practical point of view. If the House is big enough to contain all its Members, nine-tenths of its Debates will be conducted in the depressing atmosphere of an almost empty or half-empty Chamber. The essence of good House of Commons speaking is the conversational style, the facility for quick, informal interruptions and interchanges. Harangues from a rostrum would be a bad substitute for the conversational style in which so much of our business is done. But the conversational style requires a fairly small space, and there should be on great occasions a sense of crowd and urgency. There should be a sense of the importance of much that is said and a sense that great matters are being decided, there and then, by the House. (*Hansard*, HC Deb., 23 October 1943, vol. 393, col. 403).

28. See Jamin B. Raskin, "Legal Aliens, Local Citizens: The Historical, Constitutional and Theoretical Meanings of Alien Suffrage," *University of Pennsylvania Law Review* 141 (1993): 1391–70.

29. Ibid., 1405.

30. *Spheres of Justice: A Defense of Pluralism and Equality* (New York: Basic Books, 1983), 62.

31. See his discussion in chapter 3 of *The Ethics of Immigration* (Oxford: Oxford University Press, 2013); on p. 60, he accepts that a country might legitimately require up to ten years residence before granting citizenship on an immigrant.

32. As Sen observed, the aggregation of *opinion* is the essence of Arrow's theorem, though the implications of this are often overlooked. "Welfare Inequalities and Rawlsian Axiomatics" in *Foundational Problems in the Special Sciences* ed. Robert E. Butts and Jaakko Hintikka (Dordrecht: D. Reidel, 1975), 284.

33. Kenneth J. Arrow, *Social Choice and Individual Values*, 2nd ed. (New Haven, CT: Yale University Press, 1963), 7.

34. "[T]he belief in democracy may be so strong that any decision on the distribution of goods arrived at democratically may be preferred to such a decision arrived at in other ways, even though all individuals might have preferred the second distribution of goods to the first if it had been arrived at democratically." (Footnote: "Cf. Rousseau . . . : 'The law of plurality of votes is itself established by agreement, and supposes unanimity at least in the beginning.'") Arrow concluded that this "would require that individuals ascribe an incommensurably greater value to the process than to the decisions reached under it, a proposition which hardly seems like a credible representation of the psychology of most individuals in a social situation" (*Social Choice and Individual Values*, 90–91). But something like this has to be true of genuine democrats. Obviously democratic voting can in theory produce horrendous results, but so can any sublunary institution; the democrat will accept as legitimate any decisions made by the majority, up to the point at which the state he is in has (in his eyes) no legitimacy over him at all because of the character of the decision. But a democrat cannot balance the greater benefit of some policy against the fact that it was decided undemocratically—reasoning of that kind is the classic way democracies fall, or are "usurped," to use Rousseau's language. Arrow also thought that Rousseau was an epistemic democrat (p. 85 and n. 24), something he may have been the first to suggest; he traced a version of epistemic democracy back to Frank H. Knight's 1935 essay "Economic Theory and Nationalism," in *The Ethics of Competition and Other Essays* (New York: Harper & Brothers, 1935), 277–359.

35. Hobbes, who had thought deeply about these questions, once remarked in a fascinating letter to one of his pupils in the Cavendish household (who was planning to fight a duel in Paris over a frivolous love affair) that "I think it no ill Counsell, that you professe no loue to any woman which you hope not to marry or otherwise to enioy. For an action without designe is that which all the world calles Vanity." Vanity or vainglory, for Hobbes, was the prime source of political as well as personal evils, precisely because it was irresponsible, "action without designe". *The Correspondence of Thomas Hobbes*, vol. I, ed. Noel Malcolm (Oxford: Oxford University Press, 1994), 52. There is a profound truth here about Hobbes's politics. As far as he was concerned, one should either have one's own opinions and act on them—as in a democracy—or accept that if one cannot act on them, one should not *have* them, as in a Hobbesian monarchy. The worst thing was what he thought he saw in the England of the 1630s and 1640s: the constant airing of opinions and consequent enmity between fellow citizens, who thought that the only way to make good on their beliefs was through victory in a civil war.

NOTES TO CHAPTER 4   167

Chapter 3

1. Chapter 1 sec. I.

2. Chapter 1 sec. III.

3. Chapter 2 sec. I. For earlier development by Tuck of a conception of collective action and of an account of Rousseau as a key figure in modern democratic thought, see Richard Tuck, *Free Riding* (Cambridge, MA: Harvard University Press, 2008) and *The Sleeping Sovereign: The Invention of Modern Democracy* (Cambridge: Cambridge University Press, 2015). The claim, in the latter book, that Rousseau "accepted the practical exigencies of modern politics" is, I think, correct, and important to bear in mind in reading the discussion of Rousseau in his first chapter.

4. To be sure, participation rights must themselves be assured. So, too, must other rights—including rights of association and expression—that are required if majoritarian democracy is to be a form of active and collective self-rule. In these chapters, Tuck is surprisingly casual about what rights he thinks should be assured or how that assurance is to work.

5. Chapter 1 sec. I.

6. I present the main line of thinking in much more detail in Joshua Cohen, *Rousseau: A Free Community of Equals* (Oxford: Oxford University Press, 2010).

7. All references to *The Social Contract* will be included parenthetically in the text. See *Rousseau: The Social Contract and Other Later Political Writings*, ed. and trans. Victor Gourevitch (Cambridge: Cambridge University Press, 1997).

8. Chapter 1 sec. V.

9. Rousseau, *Letters Written from the Mountain*, in *Collected Writings of Rousseau*, vol. 9, ed. Christopher Kelly and Eve Grace, trans. Christopher Kelly and Judith R. Bush (Hanover and London: University Press of New England, 2001), p. 257.

10. Chapter 1 sec. V.

11. Chapter 1 sec. V.

12. Rousseau, *Letters Written from the Mountain*, pp. 238–39.

13. Ibid., p. 306.

Chapter 4

1. Malcolm Crook, *Elections in the French Revolution: An Apprenticeship in Democracy, 1789–1799* (Cambridge: Cambridge University Press, 1996), 38. Sieyès himself specifically estimated a sixth of the population, or 4,400,000 active citizens. Emmanuel-Joseph Sieyès, "Observations sur le rapport du Comité de constitution concernant la nouvelle organisation de la France," in *Les Archives de la Révolution française* (Versailles: Baudouin, 1789), 15; http://catalogue.bnf.fr/ark:/12148/cb37237951c (accessed January 14, 2021).

2. See Richard Tuck, *The Sleeping Sovereign: The Invention of Modern Democracy* (Cambridge: Cambridge University Press, 2016). For a longer review of *The Sleeping Sovereign* making extensive use of sleep analogies, see Jeffrey Lenowitz and Melissa Schwartzberg, "Insomnia and Other Constitutional Pathologies," *Modern Intellectual History* 16, no. 1 (April 2019): 295–308.

3. Sieyès, "Observations sur le rapport du Comité de constitution," 10–11 (my translation).

4. Jean-Antoine-Nicolas de Caritat Condorcet, *Condorcet: Foundations of Social Choice and Political Theory* (Aldershot, Hants, UK: Edward Elgar, 1994), 299.

5. Melvin Allen Edelstein, *The French Revolution and the Birth of Electoral Democracy* (Farnham, Surrey, UK: Ashgate, 2014), 44. As Adam Lindsay has recently argued, Sieyès insisted in "What Is the Third Estate?" that the nobility were the true "parasites," idle rather than economically productive. See Adam Lindsay, "Sieyès and Republican Liberty," *European Journal of Political Theory*, December 2020 (online first).

6. Crook, *Elections in the French Revolution*, 80.

7. Bernard Manin, *Principles of Representative Government* (New York: Cambridge University Press, 1997), 100–101.

8. Edelstein in fact argues that the option of limiting the suffrage to the "politically mature" was specifically rejected as antithetical to the Revolution's principles, and so the Constitutional Committee instead chose the taxation condition for suffrage, and property ownership for election to the lower chamber, to ensure that deputies would be capable of "independent judgment." Edelstein, *French Revolution*, 43–44.

9. See IV.8 in Jean-Jacques Rousseau, *The Social Contract and Other Later Political Writings* (Cambridge: Cambridge University Press, 1997) (English page citations are to this edition), 150.

10. See II.8, in ibid., 73.

11. Ibid.

12. Jean-Jacques Rousseau, *Emile; Or, On Education* (New York: Basic Books, 1979), 46.

13. Ibid., 358.

14. Ibid., 387. French edition: Jean-Jacques Rousseau, *Emile, ou De l'éducation* (Paris: Garnier, 1999), 489.

15. See I.6 in Rousseau, *Social Contract*, 51.

16. Rousseau, *Emile*, 361.

17. Ibid., 364.

18. Joan B. Landes, *Women and the Public Sphere in the Age of the French Revolution* (Ithaca, NY: Cornell University Press, 1988), 143. See also Immanuel Wallerstein, "Citizens All? Citizens Some! The Making of the Citizen," *Comparative Studies in Society and History* 45, no. 4 (2003): 654.

19. *Moniteur*, vol. 18, 17 November 1793, p. 450. Cited in Jane Abray, "Feminism in the French Revolution," *American Historical Review* 80, no. 1 (1975): 43–62, p. 57.

20. Rousseau, *Social Contract and Other Later Political Writings*, 52.

21. See IV.1, Rousseau, *Social Contract*, 122.

22. Let me also note that Rousseau is not merely a theorist of political obligation in the narrow sense of the conditions under which people ought to obey the law or accept the results of a majority vote. It is instead the link he develops between the majority vote and *autonomy*—the moral demands of self-legislation—that makes Rousseau so fascinating. There would be nothing especially interesting in the *Social Contract* if it were merely an account of how to justify majority rule; Rousseau would not need the device of the general will to provide it. And Judith Shklar would have been wrong that the concept expresses "everything that Rousseau most wanted to say." (She was not.) See Judith N. Shklar, *Men and Citizens: A Study of Rousseau's Social Theory* (Cambridge; New York: Cambridge University Press, 1985), 184.

23. Rousseau, *Social Contract*, 124.

24. Ibid.

25. Melissa Schwartzberg, "Rousseau on Fundamental Law," *Political Studies* 51, no. 2 (2003): 387–403; Melissa Schwartzberg, "Voting the General Will: Rousseau on Decision Rules," *Political Theory* 36, no. 3 (2008): 403–23.

26. See II.4 in Rousseau, *Social Contract*, 62.

27. Emmanuel Joseph Sieyès, *Political Writings: Including the Debate between Sieyès and Tom Paine in 1791* (Indianapolis, IN: Hackett, 2003), 11.

28. Ibid.

29. Lucia Rubinelli has persuasively argued that Sieyès construed the constituent power as the power to authorize the creation of the political order at extraordinary founding moments. The constituted order, in which representatives act on an ongoing basis, is not the direct expression of the popular will. The appointment of representatives allows individuals to delegate political power and conserve the time and resources for their own goals. Lucia Rubinelli, "How to Think beyond Sovereignty: On Sieyès and Constituent Power," *European Journal of Political Theory* 18, no. 1 (2016): 47–67.

30. Sieyès, *Political Writings*, 150 (italics in original).

31. James C. Scott, *Domination and the Arts of Resistance: Hidden Transcripts* (New Haven, CT: Yale University Press, 2008), 188; see also James C. Scott, *Weapons of the Weak: Everyday Forms of Peasant Resistance* (New Haven, CT: Yale University Press, 1985).

32. The first clinical use of the term "passive-aggressive" appeared in a technical bulletin issued by the US War Department (TB MD 203) in 1945 to describe soldiers who shirked their duties and refused to comply with the demands of their officers. Psychiatrist Colonel William Menninger observed soldiers using "passive measures, such as pouting, stubbornness, procrastination, inefficiency, and passive obstructionism"

against their superiors. See Christopher Lane, "The Surprising History of Passive-Aggressive Personality Disorder," *Theory & Psychology* 19, no. 1 (2009): 58. See also K. L. Malinowski, "Passive-Aggressive Personality," in J. R. Lion, ed., *Personality Disorders: Diagnosis and Management* 2nd edition (Baltimore: Williams & Wilkins, 1981), 121–32, 123; Theodore Millon, *Disorders of Personality: DSM-III, Axis II* (New York: Wiley, 1981), 247.

33. Dominique Godineau, *The Women of Paris and Their French Revolution* (Berkeley: University of California Press, 1998).

34. Anne L. Macdonald, *No Idle Hands: The Social History of American Knitting* (New York: Ballantine, 1988), 27–28.

Chapter 5

1. This passage is not only the basis for the epistemological interpretation of *The Social Contract*, but also a statement of the moral relation between each person and the body politic: every person, as citizen, has the general will as part of his or her will: "each individual . . . may have a particular will contrary or dissimilar to the general will which he has as a citizen. His particular interest may speak to him quite differently from the common interest: his absolute and naturally independent existence may make him look upon what he owes to the common cause as a gratuitous contribution, the loss of which will do less harm to others than the payment of it is burdensome to himself; and, regarding the moral person which constitutes the State as a *persona ficta*, because not a man, he may wish to enjoy the rights of citizenship without being ready to fulfil the duties of a subject. The continuance of such an injustice could not but prove the undoing of the body politic" (I.7). Evidently, Rousseau regards such free-riding as inconsistent with virtue that citizens must exhibit if they are to be free in the civil state: "man acquires in the civil state, moral liberty, which alone makes him truly master of himself; for the mere impulse of appetite is slavery, while obedience to a law which we prescribe to ourselves is liberty" (I.8).

2. That would be a matter for the law to determine.

3. As Tuck acknowledges, Rousseau opposed the liberation of the serfs on the ground that they were not prepared for self-government. He thought that only *free* men were capable of (active) citizenship, and he did not seem to think that there were many of those to be found among the serfs in Poland, nor among the slaves in the New World. He hoped that they might be educated for citizenship and, if and as this happened, admitted to citizenship by the censor. He seemed to think therefore that a litmus test was necessary and appropriate for membership in the "people." This may be analogous to Tuck's suggested immigration policy in that it admits only the worthy to full citizenship; but it seems uncomfortably similar to literacy tests, which were employed by many American states in the Jim Crow era.

4. A collectivist interpretation implies a very weak conception of group agency. It says only that the group action supervenes in a certain way on the actions of its members. Thus, when in an election, candidate A prevails by a majority vote over candidate B, we can say that the "people" have decided for A over B. An important feature of the collective conception is that it depends on institutional facts—specifically, on the voting rule in force. If the decision between A and B was to be made by weighted majority (as it would have been in the comitia centuriata in republican Rome), the fact that A had a simple majority would not necessarily have meant that the comitia chose A over B. That choice would have depended on A winning the wealth-weighted vote over B.

5. In chapter 2, he spoke critically of Hobbes's view in De Cive, "On this view, the outvoted member of an assembly is no different from a citizen who takes no part in its proceedings, nor indeed from a citizen of a country where there is no democracy: anyone who is willing to abide by the constitutional structure has given this general authority to the sovereign to act on their behalf. But if this is the basis for saying that the action of a majority is 'mine' even though I am outvoted, then by the same token, the action of the majority is 'mine' even though I did not vote at all, and that seems to undermine completely the force of the Rousseauian thought that we must all take part in an active fashion in making our laws" (chap. 2 sec. V).

6. I take Rousseau's embrace of classical examples of Rome and Sparta as supporting the collectivist interpretation. Voting in Rome was based on wide franchise (for the time) but was weighted explicitly by wealth in the Comitia Centuriata, which voted by wealth class, and implicitly by wealth in the Comitia Tributa and therefore in the plebeian assembly, which voted by tribe, as well (because the poor were mostly stacked into the four urban tribes, which rarely got the chance to have their votes count at all). And Sparta had hardly any citizens at all but was mostly populated by slaves (helots). And as I argue, his proposals for Poland essentially followed these classical examples.

7. I am unpersuaded by Tuck's arguments against the epistemic view. Tuck says "the authority of the decision rests not on the fact that the majority voted for it but on the fact it is the right course of action, and the vote is merely evidence for that, and conceivably not the only or the best kind of evidence." That seems right in two senses, which are not identical: If the majority voted for it, then it is part of the general will (or common interest), and of course that is a moral reason to take the action. But if the majority voted for it, it becomes the law, and that gives another kind of reason for doing it. These two senses can come apart. This reading makes sense of passages in The Social Contract in which Rousseau admits that the people may be deceived and fail to enact as law what the general will requires (II.3). I suppose sovereign mistakes can go either way: the people may accept as a law something that cannot be a law (because it failed to be general or for some other reason). The

Arrow-Condorcet model suggests that (under certain conditions) moral and legal authority will tend to run together (in a well-run community).

Tuck also argues that there may be other mechanisms than voting that could reliably reveal the general will (a suitably constructed public opinion poll P, for example). This is obviously true. Supposing that an individual was convinced that P was reliable, then she would have reason to conform her beliefs to the poll results. But that would not make P's result a law. Laws need to be accepted by the people in a direct vote. Plainly being part of the general will is neither necessary nor sufficient for a proposition to be law. It is a matter of probabilities (and the necessary procedures actually being followed).

8. Rousseau insisted that "There is often a great deal of difference between the will of all and the general will; the latter considers only the common interest, while the former takes private interest into account, and is no more than a sum of particular wills: but take away from these same wills the pluses and minuses that cancel one another, and the general will remains as the sum of the differences" (*Social Contract* I.3). But this would be true only when the proposition voted on is a matter of the common interest—which is an interest shared by all. In that case, the cancellation would occur because private interests would cancel out or average out, leaving the general will. But where the proposition to be voted on is an expression of the interest of a mere majority to take advantage of a minority, it is hard to see how the cancellation argument could yield the general will. There is no general will to express in that case.

9. Rousseau, like many writers in the seventeenth and eighteenth centuries, identified the power to make laws with sovereignty. A view of this kind was common to those who advocated the detachment of the legislative power from the monarch. It was embodied in the Crown-in-Parliament model established in the early eighteenth-century United Kingdom and was advocated by Montesquieu, DeLolme, and many others for other European monarchies. The same idea is reflected in the structure of the US Constitution (as well as in the earlier Articles of Confederation), where the powers of (the national) government are identified with the powers of Congress.

10. "Besides the extraordinary assemblies unforeseen circumstances may demand, there must be fixed periodical assemblies which cannot be abrogated or prorogued, so that on the proper day the people is legitimately called together by law, without need of any formal summoning. But, apart from these assemblies authorised by their date alone, every assembly of the people not summoned by the magistrates appointed for that purpose, and in accordance with the prescribed forms, should be regarded as unlawful, and all its acts as null and void, because the command to assemble should itself proceed from the law" (III.13).

11. In Geneva, the government had got rid of the regular meetings of the General Council, and Rousseau struggled to explain how the right of remonstrance might

provide a way for members of the sovereign—acting as individuals—might be able to get a General Council (the sovereign) into being by requiring the magistrates to refer remonstrances to the General Council. He regarded this right as similar to the right that Romans had to appeal to a tribune for intercession against a magistrate: a right to due process or trial before punishment.

12. The origin of this right was in a mediated settlement of an early-eighteenth-century conflict between the government and those who favored restoring legislative powers to the General Council. Rousseau argued that the government could not simply ignore remonstrances but must refer them to the General Council for consideration. This idea seemed original and, as far as I can tell, went nowhere.

13. Rousseau says at the start of III.1 (on government) that "the dominant will of the prince is, or should be, nothing but the general will or the law; his force is only the public force concentrated in his hands, and, as soon as he tries to base any absolute and independent act on his own authority, the tie that binds the whole together begins to be loosened." However, in III.2 he outlines the psychology of the magistrate (and, essentially of every citizen as well): "In the person of the magistrate we can distinguish three essentially different wills: first, the private will of the individual, tending only to his personal advantage; secondly, the common will of the magistrates, which is relative solely to the advantage of the prince, and may be called corporate will, being general in relation to the government, and particular in relation to the State, of which the government forms part; and, in the third place, the will of the people or the sovereign will, which is general both in relation to the State regarded as the whole, and to the government regarded as a part of the whole." So, the general will should regulate the actions of the government, but in fact, there is a constant struggle between it and the individual or corporate wills.

14. Quotations are from *Rousseau's Political Writings: Discourse on Inequality, Discourse on Political Economy, On Social Contract*, ed. Alan Ritter and Julia Conaway Bondanella, trans. Julia Conaway Bondanella, Norton Critical Edition (New York: W. W. Norton, 1987), 91–92.

Chapter 6

1. Simone Chambers, *Contemporary Democratic Theory* (Cambridge: Polity Press, 2023).

2. Josiah Ober, *Demopolis: Democracy before Liberalism in Theory and Practice* (Cambridge: Cambridge University Press, 2017).

3. John Gastil and Erik Olin Wright, *Legislature by Lot: Transformative Design for Deliberative Governance* (New York: Verso, 2019); Arash Abizadeh, "Representation, Bicameralism, Political Equality, and Sortition: Reconstituting the Second Chamber as a Randomly Selected Assembly," *Perspectives on Politics* 19 (2021): 791–806; Hélène

Landemore, *Open Democracy: Reinventing Popular Rule for the Twenty-First Century* (Princeton, NJ: Princeton University Press, 2020).

4. Bernard Manin, *The Principles of Representative Government* (Cambridge: Cambridge University Press, 1997).

5. Nicholas Carnes, *The Cash Ceiling: Why the Rich Run for Office—And What We Can Do about It* (Princeton: Princeton University Press, 2018).

6. Martin Gillens and Benjamin Page, *Democracy in America? What Has Gone Wrong and What We Can Do About It* (Chicago: University of Chicago Press, 2017); Jacob S. Hacker and Paul Pierson, *Winner Take-All Politics: How Washington Made the Rich Richer—and Turned Its Back on the Middle Class* (New York: Simon and Schuster, 2011).

7. Go to https://participedia.net/ to get a sample.

8. James Fishkin, *Democracy when the People Think: Revitalizing our Politics through Public Deliberation* (Oxford: Oxford University Press, 2018); Michael Neblo, Kevin Esterling, and David Lazer, *Politics with the People* (Cambridge: Cambridge University Press, 2018).

9. John Gastil and Katherine R. Knobloch, *Hope for Democracy: How Citizens Can Bring Reason Back into Politics,* (Oxford: Oxford University Press, 2020).

10. Jan-Werner Müller, *What Is Populism?* (Philadelphia: University of Pennsylvania Press, 2016); Simone Chambers, "Democracy and Constitutional Reform: Deliberative versus Populist Constitutionalism," *Philosophy and Social Criticism* 45 (2019) 1116–31.

11. Yochai Benkler et al., "Mail-in Voter Fraud: Anatomy of a Disinformation Campaign," Berkman Klein Center for Internet & Society at Harvard University, Research Publication 2020–6 (2020), https://cyber.harvard.edu/publication/2020/Mail-in-Voter-Fraud-Disinformation-2020.

12. Simone Chambers and Jeffrey Kopstein, "Wrecking the Public Sphere: The New Authoritarian Attack on Pluralism and Truth," *Constellations* (17 May 2022), https://doi.org/10.1111/1467-8675.12620.

13. Manin, *Principles of Representative Government*, 359.

14. Melissa Schwartzberg, *Counting the Many: The Origins and Limits of Supermajority Rule* (Cambridge: Cambridge University Press, 2014).

15. John Dewey, *The Public and Its Problems* (Chicago: Swallow Press, 1954) 207–8.

16. Jane Suiter and Theresa Reidy, "Does Deliberation Help Deliver Informed Electorates: Evidence from Irish Referendum Votes," *Representation* 56 (2020) 539–57.

Chapter 7

1. Interestingly, Rousseau said just the same about the *"jurisconsultes"* in his unpublished essay "Principes du Droit de la Guerre." See *Principes du Droit de la Guerre, Écrits sur la Paix Perpétuelle*, ed. Bruno Bernardi and Gabriella Silvestrini (Paris: Librairie Philosophique J. Vrin, 2008), 69.

2. Hobbes had earlier explained that natural law forbade such things "implicitly", since "natural law . . . commands that *agreements* be kept, and hence also commands men to show obedience when they have agreed to obey, and to keep their hands off what is another's, when what is another's has been defined by civil law" (*De Cive* XIV.9).

3. There was no complete translation of *Leviathan* into French until 1971, whereas *De Cive* has been available in a French translation that Hobbes himself had approved from 1649 down to the present day. This is likely to be the version of Hobbes that Rousseau read.

4. Also quoted in n. 65 of chapter 1.

5. *The Sleeping Sovereign*, 109–10.

6. E.g., "Every one can see, in Chapters III and IV of the First Book of Grotius, how the learned man and his translator, Barbeyrac, entangle and tie themselves up in their own sophistries, for fear of saying too little or too much of what they think, and so offending the interests they have to conciliate" (*Social Contract* II.3). Barbeyrac in particular is criticized in many of Rousseau's works, and while Pufendorf is rather rarely mentioned by name, the late Robert Wokler showed persuasively how extensive was Rousseau's critique of him in "Rousseau's Pufendorf: Natural Law and the Foundations of Commercial Society," *History of Political Thought* 15, no. 3 (Autumn 1994): 373–402.

7. For an early example of this, see a work by the aged Jesuit Louis Castel:

On croiroit que M. Rousseau a beaucoup Hobbes en vue, pour le réfuter dans ce que son système a d'impie; on ne voit pourtant pas que li'impiété de Hobbes le révolte beaucoup; s'il la refute, c'est en la courant, en l'effaçant. Hobbes n'est impie, qu'en ce qu'il suppose l'homme capable d'impiété. L'homme n'ayant de soi ni verts ni vices, ni relations morales, ni devoirs connus, ne sçauroit être impie, quoi qu'il fasse, non plus que la bête brute & animale. L'homme de Hobbes est bête jusqu'à l'impiété: celui de M. Rousseau est impie jusqu'à la bêtise. Il n'est pas impie, mais il n'est pas pieuse: il n'est rien de moral. [Louis Castel], *L'homme moral opposé a l'homme physique de Monsieur R****. Lettre philosophique où l'on refute le Déisme du jour* (Toulouse, 1756), 57–58.

See also ibid., 202–4, on Rousseau as a Hobbist in religion (though it should be said that he also attacks Locke in this context), and 207ff. on Rousseau as an Epicurean—which often meant Hobbist in the seventeenth and eighteenth centuries. These criticisms were reprinted in 1784 in the *Supplement* to the Geneva edition of Rousseau's works (vol. III) and were thereby kept in full view of all the late-eighteenth- and early-nineteenth-century readers of Rousseau, including most importantly his German ones. Similar points were made in another response to the Second Discourse from 1756 by Jean de Castillon, that Rousseau's man "est méchant comme celui de Hobbes" (*Discours sur l'origine de l'inegalité parmi les hommes*

[Amsterdam, 1756], 129). Another example: in 1778 Gian-Rinaldo Carli, spokesman for the Austrian Enlightenment in Italy and influential writer on economic affairs, published *L'uomo libero* as a an appeal for respect to the law and to our parents and sovereigns, against what he called the "venomous writings" of "the ferocious *Hobbes* and the seductive *Rousseau.*" He summarized their chief failing as the fact that "by the word *liberty* they mean independence, in other words the right to do everything to everything, as Hobbes defines it, and as Rousseau understands it" (G. R. Carli, *L'uomo libero*, 2nd ed. [Venice, 1783], 7, 182; 1st ed. [Milan, 1778]). Kant, too, was fully aware of the similarity between Hobbes and Rousseau, with the profound observation in his *Lectures on Natural Right* that "So far, no one has fully understood that it is one of the first duties to enter civil society. Hobbes and Rousseau, however, have had some idea of this." See Gottfried Feyerabend, [*Notes on*] *Kant's Natural Right, Read in the Winter Semester of the Year 1784*, trans. Lars Vinx (unpublished, October 2003, available through Academia.edu), 24. I prefer Vinx's translation to the published version of the lectures, *Lectures and Drafts on Political Philosophy*, ed. Frederick Rauscher (Cambridge: Cambridge University Press, 2016).

8. See also Rousseau's remark in book II chapter 2: "We are told that the jugglers of Japan dismember a child before the eyes of the spectators; then they throw all the members into the air one after another, and the child falls down alive and whole. The conjuring tricks of our political theorists are very like that; they first dismember the body politic by an illusion worthy of a fair, and then join it together again we know not how."

9. *The Social Contract and the Discourses*, trans. G.D.H. Cole, revised and augmented J.H. Brumfitt and John C. Hall (Everyman's Library) (London: J.M. Dent 1973) pp 120–121.

10. See in particular the important but often neglected set of secondary laws of nature in chapter III of *De Cive*, such as the eighth, *everyone should be considered equal to everyone*, and the ninth, *whatever rights each claims for himself, he must also allow to everyone else*. The best discussion of this aspect of Hobbes is Kinch Hoekstra, "Hobbesian Equality" in *Hobbes Today: Insights for the 21st Century*, ed. S. A. Lloyd (Cambridge: Cambridge University Press, 2012), 76–112.

11. Joshua Cohen, *Rousseau: A Free Community of Equals* (Oxford: Oxford University Press, 2010). See in particular his discussion on pp. 68–73.

12. See *The Metaphysics of Morals*, Public Right Section I §44 in Kant, *Practical Philosophy*, ed. and trans. Mary J. Gregor (Cambridge: Cambridge University Press, 1996), 455–56.

13. I do not want here to go into the question of whether Nicholas Dent was right in his account of *a benign amour propre* in Rousseau; for criticisms of his view, see Michael Rosen, *On Voluntary Servitude: False Consciousness and the Theory of Ideology* (Cambridge, MA: Harvard University Press, 1996), 85–87 and n. 77. Certainly, it is

hard to read this account (based largely on *Emile*) into the *Social Contract* and the *Discourses*. It is noteworthy that Cohen in his book (p. 4) pays tribute to Dent's "eye-opening" account as an inspiration for his own interpretation of Rousseau.

14. Compare his remark in chapter 11 of his *Essai sur l'origine des langues*: "When we put ourselves in the position of others, we do not become what they must be, but remain ourselves, modified. And, when we think we are judging them rationally, we merely compare their prejudices to ours." (*On the Origin of Language: Jean-Jacques Rousseau, Essay on the Origin of Languages; Johann Gottfried Herder, Essay on the Origin of Language,* trans. and ed. J. H. Moran [New York: Frederick Ungar, 1966], 49).

15. *The Social Contract and the Discourses,* trans. G.D.H. Cole, rev. and aug. J. H. Brumfitt and John C. Hall, Everyman's Library (London: J. M. Dent, 1973), 298. Rousseau here attributed to Hobbes, incorrectly but in line with the conventional view of his time, the belief that the right to all things is a "right to everything"—whereas his own alternative formulation was in fact much closer to the real Hobbes, who thought that I am entitled in nature only to those things that I judge to be conducive to my self-preservation, though virtually anything may in appropriate circumstances fall into this category.

16. I.e., the members of the Royal Society. See Steven Shapin and Simon Schaffer, *Leviathan and the Air-Pump: Hobbes, Boyle, and the Experimental Life* (Princeton: Princeton University Press 1985).

17. *Social Contract* II.2, rev. Brumfitt and Hall, 184.

18. *Dire . . . sur la question du Veto Royal* [September 1789], 17–18, my translation.

19. "Up to the present the democratic Constitution has been poorly examined. All those who have spoken about it either did not know it, or took too little interest in it, or had an interest in presenting it in a false light. None of them have sufficiently distinguished the Sovereign from the Government." Eighth Letter from the Mountain, in *Oeuvres complètes,* vol. III, ed. Michel Launay (Paris: Éditions du Seuil, 1971), 465; for translation, see *Letter to Beaumont, Letters Written from the Mountain, and Related Writings,* trans. Christopher Kelly and Judith Bush, ed. Christopher Kelly and Eve Grace (Hanover, NH: University Press of New England, 2001), 257. See also my *Sleeping Sovereign,* 1–4.

20. *Sleeping Sovereign,* chap. 4.

21. "[I]f in a *Democracy* the *people* chose to concentrate deliberations about war and peace and legislation in the hands of just one man or a very small number of men, content themselves with the appointment of magistrates and public ministers, content, that is, to have authority without executive function, then it must be admitted that *Democracy* and *Monarchy* would be equal in this matter" (*De Cive* X.15; see also his remark in the *Elements* II.5.8; "aristocracy" there, as he had said in II.5.3, encompasses democracy).

22. Jeffrey Lenowitz and Melissa Schwartzberg, "Insomnia and Other Constitutional Pathologies," *Modern Intellectual History* 16 (2019): 295–308, based on Schwartzberg's contribution to a roundtable on the book at Yale in 2017.

23. *Oeuvres complètes*, vol. III, 483; *Letter to Beaumont, Letters Written from the Mountain*, 292–93.

24. For the schedule and practices of the General Council in Rousseau's time, see George Keate, *A Short Account of the Ancient History, Present Government, and Laws of the Republic of Geneva* (London, 1761), 66ff.

25. Carl Friedrich, *Constitutional Government and Politics*, 1st ed. (New York: Harper, 1937), 129.

26. Hannah Arendt, *The Origins of Totalitarianism* (New York: Harcourt Brace, 1951), 306. See also "It has frequently been pointed out that totalitarian movements use and abuse democratic freedoms in order to abolish them. This is not just devilish cleverness on the part of the leaders or childish stupidity on the part of the masses. Democratic freedoms may be based on the equality of all citizens before the law; yet they acquire their meaning and function organically only where the citizens belong to and are represented by groups or form a social and political hierarchy" (ibid.).

27. See, e.g., the papers in *Totalitarianism: Proceedings of a Conference Held at the American Academy of Arts and Sciences, March 1953*, ed. Carl J. Friedrich (Cambridge, MA: Harvard University Press, 1954), notably the keynote address by George Kennan. For the Italian origins of the term "totalitarian," see Bruno Bongiovanni and John Rugman, "Totalitarianism: The Word and the Thing," *Journal of Modern European History* 3.1 (2005): 5–17.

28. Kennan, it should be said, did refer to the First World War, but only as one among a number of other kinds of circumstances which might lead to totalitarianism (Friedrich, ed., *Totalitarianism*, 26). Arendt frequently talks about the psychic effect of the war, but she treats the effects as universal across Europe, and the war itself as to a degree the outcome of the same kinds of ideological and cultural forces in modernity which led to totalitarianism.

29. See Engels striking remarks about Georges Avenel's 1865 book *Anacharsis Cloots: L'orateur du genre humain* in a letter of 1889: "The whole French Revolution is dominated by the War of Coalition, all its pulsations depend upon it. If the allied army penetrates into France—predominant activity of the vagus nerves, violent heartbeat, revolutionary crisis. If it is driven back—predominance of the sympathetic nerves, the heartbeat becomes slower, the reactionary elements again push themselves into the foreground; the plebeians, the beginning of the later proletariat, whose energy alone has saved the revolution, are brought to reason and order" (Karl Marx and Friedrich Engels, *Selected Correspondence, 1846–1895*, ed. and trans. Dona Torr (New York: International Publishers, 1942), 457–58). Patrice Higonnet observed that this view of the Terror was most popular among republicans and

socialists such as Jaurès; he described it as an "exculpating explanation," but it is also the most obvious one, and the desire to find a deeper meaning usually indicates some kind of prior commitment to skepticism about democracy. "Terror, Trauma and the 'Young Marx' Explanation of Jacobin Politics," *Past & Present* 191, no. 1 (2006): 121–64, 127–28.

30. See, e.g., Friedrich: "parliamentary absolutism yielded to dictatorship by the simple device of reducing the membership of parliament sufficiently to give the willing or unwilling partisans of change a safe majority" (*Constitutional Government and Politics*, 129). This "simple device" was an undemocratic *coup*.

31. The Nazi war on Jews began with the Denaturalization Law of 1933 and the Citizenship Law of 1935. The first took the vote away from naturalized Jews (about a quarter of the German Jewish population), and the second from all Jews. In addition, all political parties except the Nazi Party were banned after 14 July.

32. Maybe we do not even have to imagine a scenario like this. The Weimar Constitutional Court for Prussia upheld the legality of the Nazi measures without any intimidation.

33. See the reply of Cornet Joyce to Charles I in 1647, when he arrived to seize the king from the Scots Army and put him under parliamentary control. The king said to him, "Tell me what commission you have"; Joyce pointed to the soldiers behind him, and said "the Souldiers present were his Commission" (*A letter from the Right Honourable Ed. Lord Montagu, one of the commissioners attending His Majesty. With a perfect narration of all the passages betwixt his majesty and those forces that brought him from Holdenby* [London, 1647], 4). Or the observation by Henry Parker, the chief theorist of the Parliamentary cause, in his book *The Contra-Replicant* (London, 1643): "Many men, especially Lawyers, would fain have Law alone take place in all times, but for my part I think it equally destructive to renounce reason of State, and adhere to Law in times of great extremity, as to renounce Law, & adhere to Policy in times of tranquillity. Nothing has done us more harme of late, then this opinion of adhering to Law only for our preservation" (p. 19).

34. The British Social Democrat Federation's program in 1884 included "LEGISLATION by the PEOPLE, in such wise that no project of Law shall become legally binding till accepted by the Majority of the People"; the German Social Democrats at Erfurt in 1891 called for "Direct legislation by the people by means of the initiative and referendum.... Authorities to be elected by the people; to be responsible and bound"; the Belgian Labour Party committed itself in 1893 to "elected persons to be bound by pledges.... Electorates to have the right of unseating elected persons.... Right of popular initiative and referendum in legislative, provincial communal matters"; the Austrian Social Democratic Party called in 1901 for "Direct legislation by the people by means of the initiative and referendum"; and the French Socialists in 1902 called for "Popular right of initiative and referendum.... Legal

regulation of the legislator's mandate, to be revocable by the vote of any absolute majority of his constituents." The exceptions were the ILP and the Labour Party in Britain, who either remained silent on the subject or were explicitly opposed to it (like Keir Hardie and Ramsay MacDonald). Despite this, as Barrow and Bullock observed, the Labour Party on the eve of the First World War was close to endorsing plebiscites. See R.C.K. Ensor, *Modern Socialism, as Set Forth by Socialists in Their Speeches, Writings and Programmes* (London: Harper, 1910), 303–69; and Logie Barrow and Ian Bullock, *Democratic Ideas and the British Labour Movement, 1880–1914* (Cambridge: Cambridge University Press, 1996), 271.

35. See Holger H. Herwig, "Clio Deceived: Patrotic Self-Censorship in Germany after the Great War," *International Security* 12 (1987): 5–44. Herwig made the point, inter alia, that the pervasiveness of the idea that the nations of Europe sleepwalked into the war has exercised a baleful influence on discussions about a possible third world war. He was of course influenced by Fritz Fischer's well-known revisionary history of the origins of the war: *Griff nach der Weltmacht: Die Kriegzielpolitik des kaiserlichen Deutschland 1914–1918* (Düsseldorf: Droste Verlag, 1961), translated as *Germany's Aims in the First World War*, ed. Hajo Holborn and James Joll (New York: W. W. Norton, 1967), in which the actual intentions of the German government, and its full understanding of what it had embarked on, were made clear. Despite some valid criticisms, on the whole Fischer's argument has stood the test of time, and it must at the very least be taken seriously, and the old conventional view (still widespread at a popular level) not be taken for granted.

36. See, e.g., Samuel Moyn, *Christian Human Rights* (Philadelphia: University of Pennsylvania Press, 2015).

37. The great example of this was the creation by the Attlee Government of the NHS, the distinctive feature of which was the nationalization of most of the existing hospitals, some of which had been independent foundations for centuries. Did the United Kingdom avoid modern constitutionalizing until the 1970s because radical energies were subsumed into the Labour Party rather than the Communist Party, and because Bevin was a stalwart opponent of the Soviet Union? Sympathy for communism was nevertheless a feature of postwar British socialism; the National Executive of the Labour Party in 1948 produced a centenary edition of the *Communist Manifesto* with a long introduction by Harold Laski. He ended, after quoting Attlee as saying, inter alia, "A Labour Government should make it quite plain that it will suffer nothing to hinder it in carrying out the popular will," by remarking,

> Mr. Attlee has never been himself a Marxist; but there is not a word in the sentences of his that I have quoted which could not have been eagerly accepted by the authors of the Communist Manifesto; and they would, I think, have inferred from them that in the degree to which the first Labour Government with a majority puts the spirit of those phrases into operation, it would fulfil

the great objectives for which it was formed. (*Communist Manifesto: Socialist Landmark; A New Appreciation Written for the Labour Party* [London: Allen and Unwin, 1948], 102–3)

38. *Les Discours de Sieyès dans les débats constitutionnels de l'an III*, ed. Paul Bastid (Paris: Librairie Hachette, 1939), 17, my translation.

39. "The electioneering mentality of democracy has disappeared and the idea of political representation has been enlarged to include every means whereby popular sentiments and aspirations are revealed, with the result that old parties have been eliminated and all political forces have been concentrated in Fascism. It was hence necessary that a new organ should arise alongside the government, and that one of its functions should be to constitute the national representative body. It is thus that the Grand Council of Fascism designates the representatives of the nation" (*Il Resto di Carlino* [at the time a Fascist newspaper], 4 December 1932, quoted in Gaetano Salvemini, "Totalitarian 'Elections' in Italy Today," *Social Research* 4 [1937]: 113).

40. *Report of the Royal Commission Appointed to Enquire Into Electoral Systems* (London: HMSO, 1910), 34. They also remarked, "It may be desirable to offer the elector a wider choice, though the popularity of the change is doubtful, as the British elector loves above all things a square fight between two men" (p. 29).

41. See, e.g., Dave Denison, "Defeating the Voters," *Baffler*, 14 May 2019.

42. See e.g. John Goldthorpe, "Social Class Mobility in Modern Britain: Changing Structure, Constant Process," *Journal of the British Academy* 4 (2016): 95–96.

43. R. Foa and Y. Mounk, "The Signs of Deconsolidation," *Journal of Democracy* 28 (2017): 5–16.

44. Amy C. Alexander and Christian Welzel, "The Myth of Deconsolidation: Rising Liberalism and the Populist Reaction," web exchange in *Journal of Democracy* (2017) at https://www.journalofdemocracy.org/wp-content/uploads/2018/12/Journal-of-Democracy-Web-Exchange-Alexander-and-Welzel.pdf.

CONTRIBUTORS

RICHARD TUCK is the Frank G. Thomson Professor of Government at Harvard University. His many books include *The Sleeping Sovereign: The Invention of Modern Democracy; Hobbes: A Very Short Introduction;* and *Natural Rights Theories: Their Origin and Development.*

JOSHUA COHEN is on the faculty at Apple University and is Distinguished Senior Fellow in Law, Philosophy, and Political Science at the University of California, Berkeley. He is co-editor-in-chief of *Boston Review,* author of *Rousseau: A Free Community of Equals,* and co-editor of *The Norton Introduction to Philosophy.*

MELISSA SCHWARTZBERG is Silver Professor of Politics at New York University. She is the author of *Democracy and Legal Change* and *Counting the Many: The Origins and Limits of Supermajority Rule,* and co-author (with Jack Knight) of the forthcoming *Democratic Deals: A Defense of Political Bargaining.* She has received fellowships from the Guggenheim Foundation, the Mellon Foundation, and the American Council of Learned Societies, as well as Princeton's University Center for Human Values.

JOHN FEREJOHN is Samuel Tilden Professor of Law at New York University. He has authored articles and books in political science, legal theory, philosophy, and economics and is a member of the American Academy of Arts and Sciences and the National Academy of Sciences.

SIMONE CHAMBERS is Professor of Political Science at the University of California, Irvine. She has written and published on such topics as deliberative democracy, referendums, constitutional politics, the public sphere, secularism, rhetoric, civility, and digital misinformation. She is the author of *Contemporary Democratic Theory* and *Reasonable Democracy: Jürgen Habermas and the Politics of Discourse*, as well as co-editor of *Alternative Conceptions of Civil Society* (with Will Kymlicka) and *Deliberation, Democracy, and the Media* (with Anne Costain).

STEPHEN MACEDO is the Laurance S. Rockefeller Professor of Politics and the former director of the University Center for Human Values at Princeton University. His books include *Liberal Virtues: Citizenship, Virtue, and Community in Liberal Constitutionalism*, *Diversity and Distrust: Civic Education in a Multicultural Democracy*, the coauthored *Democracy at Risk: How Political Choices Undermine Citizen Participation, and What We Can Do about It*, and *Just Married: Same-Sex Couples, Monogamy, and the Future of Marriage* (Princeton). He is a member of the American Academy of Arts and Sciences.

INDEX

abortion, 6; politics of, 57

active, meaning of, 149n4

active citizen(s), 74; competence checks on, 85; passive and, 2, 17, 27, 44, 68, 82, 85

active citizenship: and authorization and collective action, 112–17; and common good, 79; free man as capable of, 97, 170n3; importance of, 79–80; and majority decisions, 80; and majority view, 114–15; as marriage of procedure and substance, 74; and priority of general will, 79; Tuck on, 107; Tuck on conception of, 93–96; and universal suffrage, 113–14; and voting, 112–13

active democracy, 24, 65; meaning of, 29; moral principle of, 9; principle of, 95; Tuck on, 4

all other things being equal, principle of, 55

altruism, 54; agentive, 163n12

American political system, 131

American South, Reconstruction in, 57

anarchism, 97, 136

Arendt, Hannah, 138; on despotic regimes, 138; as German refugee, 140; *The Origins of Totalitarianism*, 138, 178n26

aristocracy, 46, 59, 97, 100, 177n21

Aristotle, 122, 123; on appointment of magistrates, 46, 48

Arrow, Kenneth: on general will, 32; impossibility theorem and, 66–67; *Social Choice and Individual Values*, 32; on voting and the market, 51

Assembly of Notables (France), 30

Australia: abstention option, 137

Austrian Enlightenment, 176n7

Austrian Social Democratic Party, 179n34

authoritarianism, 113; and authoritarian populism, 138

authority, political, 36

authority of law, universality of, 58

authorization: collective action and, 112–17; voting in collective process of, 112–13

Babeufists, 22

bandwagon effect, 56

Barbeyrac, Jean, 122, 123, 175n6

bargaining, 56

Bastille, storming of, 63, 64

Beitz, Charles, 15

Belgian Labour Party, 179n34

benefactors, recipients of charity and, 43, 161–62n77

collective action, 45; authorization
and, 112–17; logic of, 103; Tuck on,
100–101
collectivist interpretation: and group
agency, 97, 171n4; Rome and Sparta
as examples of, 171n6
common good, Rousseau linking general will and, 75–76
Communist Manifesto, 180n37
Communist Party, 141
community, Walzerian, 66
competence check, for active citizens, 85
Condorcet, Jean-Antoine-Nicolas de
Caritat, Marquis de: on exclusion of
women, 84; on the necessity of a
ratification on the constitution by
the citizens, 60–61
Constant, Benjamin, on Sieyès, 20–21
Conti, Greg, 15
Coptic Church, pope of, 162n2
corporate identity, 61, 164–65n23
cuique suum, and right of property, 129
cultural power, 129

debt, 62
Declaration of Rights, and "Citizen
Sieyès", 17
deliberation, general will and, of
people, 34–35
democracy, 1, 12; as active agent of
self-determination, 117; agentive
view of, 67; belief in, 166n34; civil
society as, 124; and decisions by
agreement of majority, 34, 160n65;
and deliberations about war and
peace, 131, 177n21; deliberative, 109,
130; electioneering mentality of,
181n39; elections in, 111; epistemic
theories of, 4; illiberal, 57, 113;

importance of procedure and substance in, 78; "liberal", 57; liberal
constitutional, 3; Lincoln describing,
as procedural and substantive, 81;
majoritarian, 58–59; in one country,
principle of, 95; political parties in,
111; Pufendorf on, 33; representation
in, 45–46; Rousseau on, 32, 77, 147;
sortition and deliberative, 109–10;
spirit of, 42–43; turning into despotism, 39; "ultra-radical" majoritarian
conception of, 5
Demosthenes, 164n20
Dent, Nicholas, 176–77n13
despotism, 39, 161n72; populist,
143
Dewey, John, on majority rule, 115
Dickens, Charles, A Tale of Two Cities,
91
division of labor, 19; political representation and, 20–21
Downs, Anthony, on voting and the
market, 51
Dudley, Soren, 16

Eisgruber, Christopher, 16
elections, recall, 94. See also voting
Engels, Friedrich, 22, 139; The Holy
Family (Marx and Engels), 21–22,
151n17
England. See United Kingdom
epistemic democracy, general will and,
32
epistemic security, 128
equality: epistemic theory and, 49; as
essential principle among citizens,
46; of rights, 24; in voting, 95
European Union (EU): authoritarian
populists against, 142; United Kingdom's exit (Brexit) from, 116–17

THE UNIVERSITY CENTER FOR
HUMAN VALUES SERIES
Stephen Macedo, Editor

A NOTE ON THE TYPE

This book has been composed in Arno, an Old-style serif typeface in the
classic Venetian tradition, designed by Robert Slimbach at Adobe.